A HUMAN IS A COMPLICATED BEING

STUCK SOMEWHERE BUT THINKING ELSEWHERE

AMARNATH AKKI

Copyright © Amarnath Akki
All Rights Reserved.

ISBN 979-888569124-6

This book is dedicated to all my dedicated readers, well wishers, motivational people who guided me through my difficult phases in my life and come through my own evil thoughts to establish some landmark in my small mortal life.

To my lovely and loving parents,

To my friends who supported me throughout the journey of this book.

To my brothers and sisters for encouraging me to do my best in delivering a masterpiece.

To my extended family and friends.

Contents

Contents

Contents

Preface

Human is very possesive over selecting his/her type of person in their individual lives by giving their every soul , energy into it.

What we really want from someone cannot be expected as gained through some small sacrifies which we do to outcome the end result of any given situation.

Why wouldn't we want to explore all kind of personalities in any given circumstance while we go into any specific goal?

Wouldn't be a crime for us to be more selfless , selfish to not want anyone to take our dream in a snap of a finger.

I startred writing articles with few given headings from the past 5 to 7 months , had to speak with nearly 100 to 150 people about their mindset, perspective, perception of why they would want to decide to enact or behave in a way which people would get hurt?

It took me almost 4 months to write these full book completely, along with this i took three weeks to edit it's final cut and produce in front of your eyes.

Acknowledgements

I would like to thank notionpress.com for publishing my three books previously , this will be my 4th book in total.

Special mention to their editioral team for their extra guidance and support my 4th dream project well before in time.

Prologue

Who would want to lead a happy life without any stress in their daily living in this existence?

Brace yourselves , I am very much confident that all your worries, difficulties , problems will vanish in the air after reading this book.

Tensions, suffocations, toxic relationships , fluctuating mind , disturbance in the soul over selecting the right set of people in our very lives just to implement or execute the right amount of energy, time , soul into whatever we wish to get succeded in our lives.

How can one be so confident without any hesitations in a specific targeted ambition which he/she would want to get their hands on victory which will be long time pending for them.

CHAPTER ONE

Human Evolution

It's been almost over 4 million years until now that we have started to walk on our legs, few more important human characteristics such as brain, the ability to make and use tools, and storing the large capacity of language. Many complex symbolic expressions art and elaborate cultural diversity emerged mainly during the last 100,000 years.

Everyone knows science , so I can't explain you more about it because for that there are so much books , search engines for it .

We have all come a long way isn't it? So let me take you back to how our ancestors lived back then.

Early Humans didn't have any hospitals for delivery of a child, any hospital either for animal attack , they all dependent only on Ayurveda medicine for everyone.

For one liners I can say humans of early age weren't delicate as of now .

Thinking was there to them but only of that day as to which animal to hunt down and eat , but nowadays we are thinking way too ahead from us and forgetting the joy of being happy at the moment by living it.

There were no online shopping apps nor shopping malls to choose from, as all roamed with freedom of being "naked", just as their thoughts too, but now we judge that if someone is even half naked.

The reality of truth is we all get naked in front of ourselves through mirror , while taking bath , in washrooms , in many ways but we all deny to accept it that we all free from hiding and accept some truthfulness in the process.

We were born in this universe naked and we all go away naked , there is no point of getting the word "shame" here , because we all lost it when we judge a person by their dress.

Those times there were no electric induction cook top, nor gas and stove but all was barbeque or eating it raw just can be even categorized with the dressing too.

Now that we are living in this modern world ,as transformed robots we don't have time for anything , everything is being hurried up or done instantly.

Competition is not allowing us to settle down in a place and have our food properly, we all are scared including me that what if I waste on more minute of mine I will lose my position in my life that may be in his employment or in any carrier ,well there will be a person who will be a better version of you always out there in the world.

The best will also get defeated by his better version of another person.

Overthinking has gotten us in very bad shape currently in our lives , so at last we should ask ourselves is it required to think this much and strain your mind , is this necessary now?

Tell your mind that I have to just stop being without work , if you are without any work and sitting idle at few places then the thought of overthinking will definitely win over your mind, so we should get busy with any sort of work which will stop us from overthinking.

But even while we are working , the thought of overthinking strikes us again and again about how can I grow if I'm at 3 level how can I reach 100000level?

Think but don't stress about thinking more about your past or future,because all you have got is "now".

You don't know what's going to happen next or you can't change your past by time travel, so just let go of it and tell your minds is this necessary now?

We think we are the intelligent ones but are we really?

Not everyone is intelligent , nor everyone is dumb . Sometimes the police gets played by thief as dumb , other times the thief is being played dumb by police.

We think we are Immortals but in reality we will get to know that we will also get hurt, we shall also bleed blood, we can also be dead in accidents, even our hearts can also be broken.

Why do we think only we are just perfect by all means ?

Nobody is or was born perfect, each and everyone who is living in this existence learns a small lesson each day or listens to one, because life has so much meaning in it .But the biggest lesson in life is we should never stop learning until nature tells us to stop.

Value:

We all just don't care as in who suffers or who goes through hardship because deep down somewhere we all want to enjoy someone's suffering , we act as a mere spectator just as nature rather than helping each other out. We enjoy the phase when someone pleads for their help.

We deny it without giving a thought of what the consequence may be but if that problem arises for us then we actually realize how important it is for one to help and

give value to people .
We will only get to know each other when we stand in their position and plead for help!
It's time to end all people sufferings from their life there would be only solution to it by giving value to it or them, because in this world all we have got is ourselves to help out, if you help a person today then the same person will give some value and help you out of the situation.
Life is a circle , it may start somewhere but it will pass through you one day.
Laugh:
We all show our beautiful teeth to someone by pinpointing out them as losers but what are we ?
We are much more big losers because all we are standing and showing them as loser but they at least tried in their life , we are just wasting our time, energy by telling someone's mistake but have we pinpointed ourselves about what mistakes we have been doing and how to rectify it?
We just want a free show where we get entertainment for free and leaving others with too many problems rather than giving ourselves that extra time to correct our self.
It is so easy to say , hey you are doing it wrong but we don't tell how to do it the right way , some can tell but many do is only complain about failing rather than teaching ourselves and other success.
Today you might be at someone but the same thing will happen back to us while some stranger would definitely do the same thing which you are doing it today , now.
It's time finally we change this behavior from including me to each and everyone who is reading this to change this from their life.

How the pain and react can take over you will only be realized only when someone complains over you, it all comes to you how to take it and the pain will only feel that time , would definitely understand how it will be to make fun of others.

Social media:

The only question lies between us is how did the earlier humans survive so many years and why are we dying so soon?

Peace of mind was there back then with earlier humans because they weren't having any social media accounts such as Facebook, Twitter, Instagram, YouTube and many more apps. There was no such limitation, temptation or any desire to humans of earlier stage because one reason they wasn't any phone, so there was no distraction from reality to a dream land where our social media land us into, as it gets very difficult to get back to reality once we are in social media.

"The most important people in our lives doesn't really live in our fantasy world"

Real people in our lives travels from a real world in reality.

We really don't speak much with the people of daily struggle nor share any real problems which is happening , but we tend to get people help us who are non – existent from social media , just ask yourself! You will get your answer.

Sometimes we actually forget who we are and start running away from facing the reality of truth , because we are scared to face it of losing it and so we try to become someone who we are not, later one some person wakes us up and tells us that this isn't you and you are heading in a wrong way to your destination.

Hence we start going back to the track where we came from rather than following some other's path to victory.

If one problem goes away after hurting us , next second there will be a bigger problem to fight for . We have to be like warrior to face the war anytime , any second with anyone either with elephant ,The king himself, or the soldier, or the horse.

Adjustment is very easy to tell but actually carrying that forward in our lives is very challenging and we end up losing it most of the times making our life messy & miserable , we all want a shortcut road so we can easily reach our destination without any hesitation so we can save time.

Shortcuts is nothing but just as an ointment to our injuries , where instantly it will take all the pain away and give us a cool effect over it, rather than we going through that pain of burning , we shall get an easy pass from suffering.

Just as everyone who took vaccine might think we are safe and no virus can kill us but even though we are vaccinated we are still mortal humans not immortal.

Adjusting to a situation is as hard as losing our ego.

Nature is just a spectator in our lives:

A dog is the King/Queen of their own road or house , it makes sure of nothing happens to the people who takes care of it or residing near it. It is a good listener of what everyone's doing and it is a keen observer of all the things.

A dog doesn't react until and unless some suspicious happens near them , it calls out to other dogs as in unity to bark , because of caution nor a warning sign so to move away.

It takes care of the whole road while they divide and take places by their wish , as the sun rises their job just finishes and they go into their nap but as some sound enters the background. The warrior inside the dog rises up with a sleepy head blinking to see who has become but automatically the mouth starts to fight with it's barking.

A squirrel which is actually a tiny creature but acts very responsible for it's survival as it keeps searching for something but ends up getting nothing .

Just as us humans , we do the same right by telling ourselves there is something even in dead-end.

Squirrel is actually very scared even of the tiny movements of any thing or any person as it runs away far away and comes again to the scene only when it feels safe , we some people in nature are some just as them only right ? Think!

A tree which is withstanding all the pain by the strength of it's roots which is very strongly grounded and it is not moving from one place to another , why also we can't withstand our problems with laying a strong foundation in our lives , and even we have to hold on to only one place/person no matter what the situation is the rainy season, the spring season or the summer.

In between all this how a person who is old in their age reacts when there is a new born baby in their family , they all put their love, priority over it and they find their happiness in them.

Do we humans of all categories always put our love/ happiness on other beings?

Even though how much ever we grow in our professional life , we all go back to a place where we all want to feel vulnerable and get settled in our lives and have children but act as if we really don't want any

restriction ? Is it true?
One fine day we will be on our death beds, but today we are sleeping with our blankets on and which is making us cozy , warmer. But tomorrow we don't know if we might or may not end up in dead bed , so all we have is "now" to achieve something small or love or to earn some respect so that there will be no regret for you later on that I didn't give it a try.

Is it that I am pushing you on a negative scale in our lives that we all die and keep fearing when the time comes or either you can think in this way as in there is this extra second, minute, day or a week that we can at least try to do something good and be grateful for every extra time given by the creation of all.

Why we all want to win in our lives , we all want our families only to be safe & happy?

Selfish thinking makes us think that we should somehow just win and that is the definition to a life, I would consider it as a wrong answer because with every failed opportunity there is a new room opening (opportunity) up for you which you haven't still seen , so remember every failed step is a experience to you to reach greater height.

This comes under possessive behavior where no one should talk to our family and create some doubts about them in us , and we say only that we should only win but this whole society is our family which is one called as humans . We are one family not the family with our surname attached to it, but all living humans together without any category filled in with.

Why we always talk to ourselves very silently , because in us there is a defender present inside us who protects us from not reaction to any stupid questions , replies to the person in a way that we don't get hurt mentally and he makes sure he is always protecting ourselves & keeping himself busy over the process of planning of what to do, when to do and how to do.

It's been almost over 4 million years until now that we have started to walk on our legs, few more important human characteristics such as brain, the ability to make and use tools, and storing the large capacity of language.

Many complex symbolic expressions art and elaborate cultural diversity emerged mainly during the last 100,000 years.

Everyone knows science , so I can't explain you more about it because for that there are so much books , search engines for it .

We have all come a long way isn't it? So let me take you back to how our ancestors lived back then.

Early Humans didn't have any hospitals for delivery of a child, any hospital either for animal attack , they all dependent only on Ayurveda medicine for everyone.

For one liners I can say humans of early age weren't delicate as of now .

Thinking was there to them but only of that day as to which animal to hunt down and eat , but nowadays we are thinking way too ahead from us and forgetting the joy of being happy at the moment by living it.

There were no online shopping apps nor shopping malls to choose from, as all roamed with freedom of being "naked", just as their thoughts too, but now we judge that if someone is even half naked.

The reality of truth is we all get naked in front of ourselves through mirror , while taking bath , in washrooms , in many ways but we all deny to accept it that we all free from hiding and accept some truthfulness in the

process.
We were born in this universe naked and we all go away naked , there is no point of getting the word "shame" here , because we all lost it when we judge a person by their dress.

Those times there were no electric induction cook top, nor gas and stove but all was barbeque or eating it raw just can be even categorized with the dressing too.

Now that we are living in this modern world ,as transformed robots we don't have time for anything , everything is being hurried up or done instantly.

Competition is not allowing us to settle down in a place and have our food properly, we all are scared including me that what if I waste on more minute of mine I will lose my position in my life that may be in his employment or in any carrier ,well there will be a person who will be a better version of you always out there in the world.

The best will also get defeated by his better version of another person.

Overthinking has gotten us in very bad shape currently in our lives , so at last we should ask ourselves is it required to think this much and strain your mind , is this necessary now?

Tell your mind that I have to just stop being without work , if you are without any work and sitting idle at few places then the thought of overthinking will definitely win over your mind, so we should get busy with any sort of work which will stop us from overthinking.

But even while we are working , the thought of overthinking strikes us again and again about how can I grow if I'm at 3 level how can I reach 100000level?

Think but don't stress about thinking more about your past or future,because all you have got is "now".

You don't know what's going to happen next or you can't change your past by time travel, so just let go of it and tell your minds is this necessary now?

We think we are the intelligent ones but are we really?

Not everyone is intelligent , nor everyone is dumb . Sometimes the police gets played by thief as dumb , other times the thief is being played dumb by police.

We think we are Immortals but in reality we will get to know that we will also get hurt, we shall also bleed blood, we can also be dead in accidents, even our hearts can also be broken.

Why do we think only we are just perfect by all means ?

Nobody is or was born perfect, each and everyone who is living in this existence learns a small lesson each day or listens to one, because life has so much meaning in it .But the biggest lesson in life is we should never stop learning until nature tells us to stop.

Value:

We all just don't care as in who suffers or who goes through hardship because deep down somewhere we all want to enjoy someone's suffering , we act as a mere spectator just as nature rather than helping each other out. We enjoy the phase when someone pleads for their help.

We deny it without giving a thought of what the consequence may be but if that problem arises for us then we actually realize how important it is for one to help and give value to people .

We will only get to know each other when we stand in their position and plead for help!

It's time to end all people sufferings from their life there would be only solution to it by giving value to it or them, because in this world all we have got is ourselves to help out, if you help a person today then the same person will give some value and help you out of the situation.

Life is a circle , it may start somewhere but it will pass through you one day.

Laugh:

We all show our beautiful teeth to someone by pinpointing out them as losers but what are we ?

We are much more big losers because all we are standing and showing them as loser but they at least tried in their life , we are just wasting our time, energy by telling someone's mistake but have we pinpointed ourselves about what mistakes we have been doing and how to rectify it?

We just want a free show where we get entertainment for free and leaving others with too many problems rather than giving ourselves that extra time to correct our self.

It is so easy to say , hey you are doing it wrong but we don't tell how to do it the right way , some can tell but many do is only complain about failing rather than teaching ourselves and other success.

Today you might be at someone but the same thing will happen back to us while some stranger would definitely do the same thing which you are doing it today , now.

It's time finally we change this behavior from including me to each and everyone who is reading this to change this from their life.

How the pain and react can take over you will only be realized only when someone complains over you, it all comes to you how to take it and the pain will only feel that time , would definitely understand how it will be to make fun of others.

Social media:

The only question lies between us is how did the earlier humans survive so many years and why are we dying so soon?

Peace of mind was there back then with earlier humans because they weren't having any social media accounts such as Facebook, Twitter, Instagram, YouTube and many more apps. There was no such limitation, temptation or any desire to humans of earlier stage because one reason they wasn't any phone, so there was no distraction from reality to a dream land where our social media land us into, as it gets very difficult to get back to reality once we are in social media.

"The most important people in our lives doesn't really live in our fantasy world"

Real people in our lives travels from a real world in reality.

We really don't speak much with the people of daily struggle nor share any real problems which is happening , but we tend to get people help us who are non – existent from social media , just ask yourself! You will get your answer.

Sometimes we actually forget who we are and start running away from facing the reality of truth , because we are scared to face it of losing it and so we try to become someone who we are not, later one some person wakes us up and tells us that this isn't you and you are heading in a wrong way to your destination.

Hence we start going back to the track where we came from rather than following some other's path to victory.

If one problem goes away after hurting us , next second there will be a bigger problem to fight for . We have to be like warrior to face the war anytime , any second with anyone either with elephant ,The king himself, or the soldier, or the horse.

Adjustment is very easy to tell but actually carrying that forward in our lives is very challenging and we end up losing it most of the times making our life messy & miserable , we all want a shortcut road so we can easily reach our destination without any hesitation so we can save time.

Shortcuts is nothing but just as an ointment to our injuries , where instantly it will take all the pain away and give us a cool effect over it, rather than we going through that pain of burning , we shall get an easy pass from suffering.

Just as everyone who took vaccine might think we are safe and no virus can kill us but even though we are vaccinated we are still mortal humans not immortal.

Adjusting to a situation is as hard as losing our ego.

Nature is just a spectator in our lives:

A dog is the King/Queen of their own road or house , it makes sure of nothing happens to the people who takes care of it or residing near it. It is a good listener of what everyone's doing and it is a keen observer of all the things.

A dog doesn't react until and unless some suspicious happens near them , it calls out to other dogs as in unity to bark , because of caution nor a warning sign so to move away.

It takes care of the whole road while they divide and take places by their wish , as the sun rises their job just finishes and they go into their nap but as some sound enters the background. The warrior inside the dog rises up with a sleepy head blinking to see who has become but automatically the mouth starts to fight with it's barking.

A squirrel which is actually a tiny creature but acts very responsible for it's survival as it keeps searching for something but ends up getting nothing .

Just as us humans , we do the same right by telling ourselves there is something even in dead-end.

Squirrel is actually very scared even of the tiny movements of any thing or any person as it runs away far away and comes again to the scene only when it feels safe , we some people in nature are some just as them only right ? Think!

A tree which is withstanding all the pain by the strength of it's roots which is very strongly grounded and it is not moving from one place to another , why also we can't withstand our problems with laying a strong foundation in our lives , and even we have to hold on to only one place/person no matter what the situation is the rainy season, the spring season or the summer.

In between all this how a person who is old in their age reacts when there is a new born baby in their family , they all put their love, priority over it and they find their happiness in them.

Do we humans of all categories always put our love/ happiness on other beings?

Even though how much ever we grow in our professional life , we all go back to a place where we all want to feel vulnerable and get settled in our lives and have children but act as if we really don't want any restriction ? Is it true?

One fine day we will be on our death beds, but today we are sleeping with our blankets on and which is making us cozy , warmer. But tomorrow we don't know if we might or may not end up in dead bed , so all we have is "now" to achieve something small or love or to earn some respect so that there will be no regret for you later on that I didn't give it a try.

Is it that I am pushing you on a negative scale in our lives that we all die and keep fearing when the time comes or either you can think in this way as in there is this extra second, minute, day or a week that we can at least try to do something good and be grateful for every extra time given by the creation of all.

Why we all want to win in our lives , we all want our families only to be safe & happy?

Selfish thinking makes us think that we should somehow just win and that is the definition to a life, I would consider it as a wrong answer because with every failed opportunity there is a new room opening (opportunity) up for you which you haven't still seen , so remember every failed step is a experience to you to reach greater height.

This comes under possessive behavior where no one should talk to our family and create some doubts about them in us , and we say only that we should only win but this whole society is our family which is one called as humans . We are one family not the family with our surname attached to it, but all living humans together without any category filled in with.

Why we always talk to ourselves very silently , because in us there is a defender present inside us who protects us from not reaction to any stupid questions , replies to the person in a way that we don't get hurt mentally and he makes sure he is always protecting ourselves & keeping himself busy over the process of planning of what to do, when to do and how to do.

It's been almost over 4 million years until now that we have started to walk on our legs, few more important human characteristics such as brain, the ability to make and use tools, and storing the large capacity of language. Many complex symbolic expressions art and elaborate cultural diversity emerged mainly during the last 100,000 years.

Everyone knows science , so I can't explain you more about it because for that there are so much books , search engines for it .

We have all come a long way isn't it? So let me take you back to how our ancestors lived back then.

Early Humans didn't have any hospitals for delivery of a child, any hospital either for animal attack , they all dependent only on Ayurveda medicine for everyone.

For one liners I can say humans of early age weren't delicate as of now .

Thinking was there to them but only of that day as to which animal to hunt down and eat , but nowadays we are thinking way too ahead from us and forgetting the joy of being happy at the moment by living it.

There were no online shopping apps nor shopping malls to choose from, as all roamed with freedom of being "naked", just as their thoughts too, but now we judge that if someone is even half naked.

The reality of truth is we all get naked in front of ourselves through mirror , while taking bath , in washrooms , in many ways but we all deny to accept it that we all free from hiding and accept some truthfulness in the process.

We were born in this universe naked and we all go away naked , there is no point of getting the word "shame" here , because we all lost it when we judge a person by their dress.

Those times there were no electric induction cook top, nor gas and stove but all was barbeque or eating it raw just can be even categorized with the dressing too.

Now that we are living in this modern world ,as transformed robots we don't have time for anything , everything is being hurried up or done instantly.

Competition is not allowing us to settle down in a place and have our food properly, we all are scared including me that what if I waste on more minute of mine I will lose my position in my life that may be in his employment or in any carrier ,well there will be a person who will be a better version of you always out there in the world.

The best will also get defeated by his better version of another person.

Overthinking has gotten us in very bad shape currently in our lives , so at last we should ask ourselves is it required to think this much and strain your mind , is this necessary now?

Tell your mind that I have to just stop being without work , if you are without any work and sitting idle at few places then the thought of overthinking will definitely win over your mind, so we should get busy with any sort of work which will stop us from overthinking.

But even while we are working , the thought of overthinking strikes us again and again about how can I grow if I'm at 3 level how can I reach 100000level?

Think but don't stress about thinking more about your past or future,because all you have got is "now".

You don't know what's going to happen next or you can't change your past by time travel, so just let go of it and tell your minds is this necessary now?

We think we are the intelligent ones but are we really?

Not everyone is intelligent , nor everyone is dumb .
Sometimes the police gets played by thief as dumb , other
times the thief is being played dumb by police.
We think we are Immortals but in reality we will get to
know that we will also get hurt, we shall also bleed blood,
we can also be dead in accidents, even our hearts can also
be broken.
Why do we think only we are just perfect by all means
?
Nobody is or was born perfect, each and everyone who
is living in this existence learns a small lesson each day or
listens to one, because life has so much meaning in it .But
the biggest lesson in life is we should never stop learning
until nature tells us to stop.
Value:
We all just don't care as in who suffers or who goes
through hardship because deep down somewhere we all
want to enjoy someone's suffering , we act as a mere
spectator just as nature rather than helping each other out.
We enjoy the phase when someone pleads for their help.
We deny it without giving a thought of what the
consequence may be but if that problem arises for us then
we actually realize how important it is for one to help and
give value to people .
We will only get to know each other when we stand in
their position and plead for help!
It's time to end all people sufferings from their life
there would be only solution to it by giving value to it or
them, because in this world all we have got is ourselves to
help out, if you help a person today then the same person
will give some value and help you out of the situation.
Life is a circle , it may start somewhere but it will pass
through you one day.

Laugh:
We all show our beautiful teeth to someone by pinpointing out them as losers but what are we ?
We are much more big losers because all we are standing and showing them as loser but they at least tried in their life , we are just wasting our time, energy by telling someone's mistake but have we pinpointed ourselves about what mistakes we have been doing and how to rectify it?
We just want a free show where we get entertainment for free and leaving others with too many problems rather than giving ourselves that extra time to correct our self.
It is so easy to say , hey you are doing it wrong but we don't tell how to do it the right way , some can tell but many do is only complain about failing rather than teaching ourselves and other success.
Today you might be at someone but the same thing will happen back to us while some stranger would definitely do the same thing which you are doing it today , now.
It's time finally we change this behavior from including me to each and everyone who is reading this to change this from their life.
How the pain and react can take over you will only be realized only when someone complains over you, it all comes to you how to take it and the pain will only feel that time , would definitely understand how it will be to make fun of others.
Social media:
The only question lies between us is how did the earlier humans survive so many years and why are we dying so soon?
Peace of mind was there back then with earlier humans because they weren't having any social media accounts

such as Facebook, Twitter, Instagram, YouTube and many more apps. There was no such limitation, temptation or any desire to humans of earlier stage because one reason they wasn't any phone, so there was no distraction from reality to a dream land where our social media land us into, as it gets very difficult to get back to reality once we are in social media.

"The most important people in our lives doesn't really live in our fantasy world"

Real people in our lives travels from a real world in reality.

We really don't speak much with the people of daily struggle nor share any real problems which is happening , but we tend to get people help us who are non – existent from social media , just ask yourself! You will get your answer.

Sometimes we actually forget who we are and start running away from facing the reality of truth , because we are scared to face it of losing it and so we try to become someone who we are not, later one some person wakes us up and tells us that this isn't you and you are heading in a wrong way to your destination.

Hence we start going back to the track where we came from rather than following some other's path to victory.

If one problem goes away after hurting us , next second there will be a bigger problem to fight for . We have to be like warrior to face the war anytime , any second with anyone either with elephant ,The king himself, or the soldier, or the horse.

Adjustment is very easy to tell but actually carrying that forward in our lives is very challenging and we end up losing it most of the times making our life messy & miserable , we all want a shortcut road so we can easily reach our destination without any hesitation so we can save time.

Shortcuts is nothing but just as an ointment to our injuries , where instantly it will take all the pain away and give us a cool effect over it, rather than we going through that pain of burning , we shall get an easy pass from suffering.

Just as everyone who took vaccine might think we are safe and no virus can kill us but even though we are vaccinated we are still mortal humans not immortal.

Adjusting to a situation is as hard as losing our ego.

Nature is just a spectator in our lives:

A dog is the King/Queen of their own road or house , it makes sure of nothing happens to the people who takes care of it or residing near it. It is a good listener of what everyone's doing and it is a keen observer of all the things.

A dog doesn't react until and unless some suspicious happens near them , it calls out to other dogs as in unity to bark , because of caution nor a warning sign so to move away.

It takes care of the whole road while they divide and take places by their wish , as the sun rises their job just finishes and they go into their nap but as some sound enters the background. The warrior inside the dog rises up with a sleepy head blinking to see who has become but automatically the mouth starts to fight with it's barking.

A squirrel which is actually a tiny creature but acts very responsible for it's survival as it keeps searching for something but ends up getting nothing .

Just as us humans , we do the same right by telling ourselves there is something even in dead-end.

Squirrel is actually very scared even of the tiny movements of any thing or any person as it runs away far away and comes again to the scene only when it feels safe , we some people in nature are some just as them only right ? Think!

A tree which is withstanding all the pain by the strength of it's roots which is very strongly grounded and it is not moving from one place to another , why also we can't withstand our problems with laying a strong foundation in our lives , and even we have to hold on to only one place/person no matter what the situation is the rainy season, the spring season or the summer.

In between all this how a person who is old in their age reacts when there is a new born baby in their family , they all put their love, priority over it and they find their happiness in them.

Do we humans of all categories always put our love/happiness on other beings?

Even though how much ever we grow in our professional life , we all go back to a place where we all want to feel vulnerable and get settled in our lives and have children but act as if we really don't want any restriction ? Is it true?

One fine day we will be on our death beds, but today we are sleeping with our blankets on and which is making us cozy , warmer. But tomorrow we don't know if we might or may not end up in dead bed , so all we have is "now" to achieve something small or love or to earn some respect so that there will be no regret for you later on that I didn't give it a try.

Is it that I am pushing you on a negative scale in our lives that we all die and keep fearing when the time comes or either you can think in this way as in there is this extra second, minute, day or a week that we can at least try to do something good and be grateful for every extra time given by the creation of all.

Why we all want to win in our lives , we all want our families only to be safe & happy?

Selfish thinking makes us think that we should somehow just win and that is the definition to a life, I would consider it as a wrong answer because with every failed opportunity there is a new room opening (opportunity) up for you which you haven't still seen , so remember every failed step is a experience to you to reach greater height.

This comes under possessive behavior where no one should talk to our family and create some doubts about them in us , and we say only that we should only win but this whole society is our family which is one called as humans . We are one family not the family with our surname attached to it, but all living humans together without any category filled in with.

Why we always talk to ourselves very silently , because in us there is a defender present inside us who protects us from not reaction to any stupid questions , replies to the person in a way that we don't get hurt mentally and he makes sure he is always protecting ourselves & keeping himself busy over the process of planning of what to do, when to do and how to do.

It's been almost over 4 million years until now that we have started to walk on our legs, few more important human characteristics such as brain, the ability to make and use tools, and storing the large capacity of language. Many complex symbolic expressions art and elaborate cultural diversity emerged mainly during the last 100,000 years.

Everyone knows science , so I can't explain you more about it because for that there are so much books , search engines for it .

We have all come a long way isn't it? So let me take you back to how our ancestors lived back then.

Early Humans didn't have any hospitals for delivery of a child, any hospital either for animal attack , they all dependent only on Ayurveda medicine for everyone.

For one liners I can say humans of early age weren't delicate as of now .

Thinking was there to them but only of that day as to which animal to hunt down and eat , but nowadays we are thinking way too ahead from us and forgetting the joy of being happy at the moment by living it.

There were no online shopping apps nor shopping malls to choose from, as all roamed with freedom of being "naked", just as their thoughts too, but now we judge that if someone is even half naked.

The reality of truth is we all get naked in front of ourselves through mirror , while taking bath , in washrooms , in many ways but we all deny to accept it that we all free from hiding and accept some truthfulness in the process.

We were born in this universe naked and we all go away naked , there is no point of getting the word "shame" here , because we all lost it when we judge a person by their dress.

Those times there were no electric induction cook top, nor gas and stove but all was barbeque or eating it raw just can be even categorized with the dressing too.

Now that we are living in this modern world ,as transformed robots we don't have time for anything , everything is being hurried up or done instantly.

Competition is not allowing us to settle down in a place and have our food properly, we all are scared including me that what if I waste on more minute of mine I will lose my position in my life that may be in his employment or in any carrier ,well there will be a person who will be a better version of you always out there in the world.

The best will also get defeated by his better version of another person.

Overthinking has gotten us in very bad shape currently in our lives , so at last we should ask ourselves is it required to think this much and strain your mind , is this necessary now?

Tell your mind that I have to just stop being without work , if you are without any work and sitting idle at few places then the thought of overthinking will definitely win over your mind, so we should get busy with any sort of work which will stop us from overthinking.

But even while we are working , the thought of overthinking strikes us again and again about how can I grow if I'm at 3 level how can I reach 100000level?

Think but don't stress about thinking more about your past or future,because all you have got is "now".

You don't know what's going to happen next or you can't change your past by time travel, so just let go of it and tell your minds is this necessary now?

We think we are the intelligent ones but are we really?

Not everyone is intelligent , nor everyone is dumb .

Sometimes the police gets played by thief as dumb , other times the thief is being played dumb by police.

We think we are Immortals but in reality we will get to know that we will also get hurt, we shall also bleed blood, we can also be dead in accidents, even our hearts can also be broken.

Why do we think only we are just perfect by all means
?

Nobody is or was born perfect, each and everyone who is living in this existence learns a small lesson each day or listens to one, because life has so much meaning in it .But the biggest lesson in life is we should never stop learning until nature tells us to stop.

Value:

We all just don't care as in who suffers or who goes through hardship because deep down somewhere we all want to enjoy someone's suffering , we act as a mere spectator just as nature rather than helping each other out. We enjoy the phase when someone pleads for their help.

We deny it without giving a thought of what the consequence may be but if that problem arises for us then we actually realize how important it is for one to help and give value to people .

We will only get to know each other when we stand in their position and plead for help!

It's time to end all people sufferings from their life there would be only solution to it by giving value to it or them, because in this world all we have got is ourselves to help out, if you help a person today then the same person will give some value and help you out of the situation.

Life is a circle , it may start somewhere but it will pass through you one day.

Laugh:

We all show our beautiful teeth to someone by pinpointing out them as losers but what are we ?

We are much more big losers because all we are standing and showing them as loser but they at least tried in their life , we are just wasting our time, energy by telling someone's mistake but have we pinpointed ourselves about what mistakes we have been doing and how to rectify it?

We just want a free show where we get entertainment for free and leaving others with too many problems rather than giving ourselves that extra time to correct our self.

It is so easy to say , hey you are doing it wrong but we don't tell how to do it the right way , some can tell but many do is only complain about failing rather than teaching ourselves and other success.

Today you might be at someone but the same thing will happen back to us while some stranger would definitely do the same thing which you are doing it today , now.

It's time finally we change this behavior from including me to each and everyone who is reading this to change this from their life.

How the pain and react can take over you will only be realized only when someone complains over you, it all comes to you how to take it and the pain will only feel that time , would definitely understand how it will be to make fun of others.

Social media:

The only question lies between us is how did the earlier humans survive so many years and why are we dying so soon?

Peace of mind was there back then with earlier humans because they weren't having any social media accounts such as Facebook, Twitter, Instagram, YouTube and many more apps. There was no such limitation, temptation or any desire to humans of earlier stage because one reason they wasn't any phone, so there was no distraction from reality to a dream land where our social media land us into, as it gets very difficult to get back to reality once we are in social media.

"The most important people in our lives doesn't really live in our fantasy world"
Real people in our lives travels from a real world in reality.
We really don't speak much with the people of daily struggle nor share any real problems which is happening , but we tend to get people help us who are non – existent from social media , just ask yourself! You will get your answer.
Sometimes we actually forget who we are and start running away from facing the reality of truth , because we are scared to face it of losing it and so we try to become someone who we are not, later one some person wakes us up and tells us that this isn't you and you are heading in a wrong way to your destination.
Hence we start going back to the track where we came from rather than following some other's path to victory.
If one problem goes away after hurting us , next second there will be a bigger problem to fight for . We have to be like warrior to face the war anytime , any second with anyone either with elephant ,The king himself, or the soldier, or the horse.
Adjustment is very easy to tell but actually carrying that forward in our lives is very challenging and we end up losing it most of the times making our life messy & miserable , we all want a shortcut road so we can easily reach our destination without any hesitation so we can save time.
Shortcuts is nothing but just as an ointment to our injuries , where instantly it will take all the pain away and give us a cool effect over it, rather than we going through that pain of burning , we shall get an easy pass from suffering.

Just as everyone who took vaccine might think we are safe and no virus can kill us but even though we are vaccinated we are still mortal humans not immortal.
Adjusting to a situation is as hard as losing our ego.
Nature is just a spectator in our lives:
A dog is the King/Queen of their own road or house , it makes sure of nothing happens to the people who takes care of it or residing near it. It is a
good listener of what everyone's doing and it is a keen observer of all the things.
A dog doesn't react until and unless some suspicious happens near them , it calls out to other dogs as in unity to bark , because of caution nor a warning sign so to move away.
It takes care of the whole road while they divide and take places by their wish , as the sun rises their job just finishes and they go into their nap but as some sound enters the background. The warrior inside the dog rises up with a sleepy head blinking to see who has become but automatically the mouth starts to fight with it's barking.
A squirrel which is actually a tiny creature but acts very responsible for it's survival as it keeps searching for something but ends up getting nothing .
Just as us humans , we do the same right by telling ourselves there is something even in dead-end.
Squirrel is actually very scared even of the tiny movements of any thing or any person as it runs away far away and comes again to the scene only when it feels safe , we some people in nature are some just as them only right ? Think!
A tree which is withstanding all the pain by the strength of it's roots which is very strongly grounded and it is not moving from one place to another , why also we

can't withstand our problems with laying a strong foundation in our lives , and even we have to hold on to only one place/person no matter what the situation is the rainy season, the spring season or the summer.

In between all this how a person who is old in their age reacts when there is a new born baby in their family , they all put their love, priority over it and they find their happiness in them.

Do we humans of all categories always put our love/ happiness on other beings?

Even though how much ever we grow in our professional life , we all go back to a place where we all want to feel vulnerable and get settled in our lives and have children but act as if we really don't want any restriction ? Is it true?

One fine day we will be on our death beds, but today we are sleeping with our blankets on and which is making us cozy , warmer. But tomorrow we don't know if we might or may not end up in dead bed , so all we have is "now" to achieve something small or love or to earn some respect so that there will be no regret for you later on that I didn't give it a try.

Is it that I am pushing you on a negative scale in our lives that we all die and keep fearing when the time comes or either you can think in this way as in there is this extra second, minute, day or a week that we can at least try to do something good and be grateful for every extra time given by the creation of all.

Why we all want to win in our lives , we all want our families only to be safe & happy?

Selfish thinking makes us think that we should somehow just win and that is the definition to a life, I would consider it as a wrong answer because with every failed opportunity there is a new room opening (opportunity) up for you which you haven't still seen , so remember every failed step is a experience to you to reach greater height.

This comes under possessive behavior where no one should talk to our family and create some doubts about them in us , and we say only that we should only win but this whole society is our family which is one called as humans . We are one family not the family with our surname attached to it, but all living humans together without any category filled in with.

Why we always talk to ourselves very silently , because in us there is a defender present inside us who protects us from not reaction to any stupid questions , replies to the person in a way that we don't get hurt mentally and he makes sure he is always protecting ourselves & keeping himself busy over the process of planning of what to do, when to do and how to do.

It's been almost over 4 million years until now that we have started to walk on our legs, few more important human characteristics such as brain, the ability to make and use tools, and storing the large capacity of language. Many complex symbolic expressions art and elaborate cultural diversity emerged mainly during the last 100,000 years.

Everyone knows science , so I can't explain you more about it because for that there are so much books , search engines for it .

We have all come a long way isn't it? So let me take you back to how our ancestors lived back then.

Early Humans didn't have any hospitals for delivery of a child, any hospital either for animal attack , they all dependent only on Ayurveda medicine for everyone.

For one liners I can say humans of early age weren't delicate as of now .

Thinking was there to them but only of that day as to which animal to hunt down and eat , but nowadays we are thinking way too ahead from us and forgetting the joy of being happy at the moment by living it.

There were no online shopping apps nor shopping malls to choose from, as all roamed with freedom of being "naked", just as their thoughts too, but now we judge that if someone is even half naked.

The reality of truth is we all get naked in front of ourselves through mirror , while taking bath , in washrooms , in many ways but we all deny to accept it that we all free from hiding and accept some truthfulness in the process.

We were born in this universe naked and we all go away naked , there is no point of getting the word "shame" here , because we all lost it when we judge a person by their dress.

Those times there were no electric induction cook top, nor gas and stove but all was barbeque or eating it raw just can be even categorized with the dressing too.

Now that we are living in this modern world ,as transformed robots we don't have time for anything , everything is being hurried up or done instantly.

Competition is not allowing us to settle down in a place and have our food properly, we all are scared including me that what if I waste on more minute of mine I will lose my position in my life that may be in his employment or in any carrier ,well there will be a person who will be a better version of you always out there in the world.

The best will also get defeated by his better version of another person.

Overthinking has gotten us in very bad shape currently in our lives , so at last we should ask ourselves is it required to think this much and strain your mind , is this necessary now?

Tell your mind that I have to just stop being without work , if you are without any work and sitting idle at few places then the thought of overthinking will definitely win over your mind, so we should get busy with any sort of work which will stop us from overthinking.

But even while we are working , the thought of overthinking strikes us again and again about how can I grow if I'm at 3 level how can I reach 100000level?

Think but don't stress about thinking more about your past or future,because all you have got is "now".

You don't know what's going to happen next or you can't change your past by time travel, so just let go of it and tell your minds is this necessary now?

We think we are the intelligent ones but are we really?

Not everyone is intelligent , nor everyone is dumb . Sometimes the police gets played by thief as dumb , other times the thief is being played dumb by police.

We think we are Immortals but in reality we will get to know that we will also get hurt, we shall also bleed blood, we can also be dead in accidents, even our hearts can also be broken.

Why do we think only we are just perfect by all means ?

Nobody is or was born perfect, each and everyone who is living in this existence learns a small lesson each day or listens to one, because life has so much meaning in it .But the biggest lesson in life is we should never stop learning until nature tells us to stop.

Value:

We all just don't care as in who suffers or who goes through hardship because deep down somewhere we all want to enjoy someone's suffering , we act as a mere spectator just as nature rather than helping each other out. We enjoy the phase when someone pleads for their help.

We deny it without giving a thought of what the consequence may be but if that problem arises for us then we actually realize how important it is for one to help and give value to people .

We will only get to know each other when we stand in their position and plead for help!

It's time to end all people sufferings from their life there would be only solution to it by giving value to it or them, because in this world all we have got is ourselves to help out, if you help a person today then the same person will give some value and help you out of the situation.

Life is a circle , it may start somewhere but it will pass through you one day.

Laugh:

We all show our beautiful teeth to someone by pinpointing out them as losers but what are we ?

We are much more big losers because all we are standing and showing them as loser but they at least tried in their life , we are just wasting our time, energy by telling someone's mistake but have we pinpointed ourselves about what mistakes we have been doing and how to rectify it?

We just want a free show where we get entertainment for free and leaving others with too many problems rather than giving ourselves that extra time to correct our self.

It is so easy to say , hey you are doing it wrong but we don't tell how to do it the right way , some can tell but many do is only complain about failing rather than teaching ourselves and other success.

Today you might be at someone but the same thing will happen back to us while some stranger would definitely do the same thing which you are doing it today , now.

It's time finally we change this behavior from including me to each and everyone who is reading this to change this from their life.

How the pain and react can take over you will only be realized only when someone complains over you, it all comes to you how to take it and the pain will only feel that time , would definitely understand how it will be to make fun of others.

Social media:

The only question lies between us is how did the earlier humans survive so many years and why are we dying so soon?

Peace of mind was there back then with earlier humans because they weren't having any social media accounts such as Facebook, Twitter, Instagram, YouTube and many more apps. There was no such limitation, temptation or any desire to humans of earlier stage because one reason they wasn't any phone, so there was no distraction from reality to a dream land where our social media land us into, as it gets very difficult to get back to reality once we are in social media.

"The most important people in our lives doesn't really live in our fantasy world"

Real people in our lives travels from a real world in reality.

We really don't speak much with the people of daily struggle nor share any real problems which is happening , but we tend to get people help us who are non – existent from social media , just ask yourself! You will get your answer.

Sometimes we actually forget who we are and start running away from facing the reality of truth , because we are scared to face it of losing it and so we try to become someone who we are not, later one some person wakes us up and tells us that this isn't you and you are heading in a wrong way to your destination.

Hence we start going back to the track where we came from rather than following some other's path to victory.

If one problem goes away after hurting us , next second there will be a bigger problem to fight for . We have to be like warrior to face the war anytime , any second with anyone either with elephant ,The king himself, or the soldier, or the horse.

Adjustment is very easy to tell but actually carrying that forward in our lives is very challenging and we end up losing it most of the times making our life messy & miserable , we all want a shortcut road so we can easily reach our destination without any hesitation so we can save time.

Shortcuts is nothing but just as an ointment to our injuries , where instantly it will take all the pain away and give us a cool effect over it, rather than we going through that pain of burning , we shall get an easy pass from suffering.

Just as everyone who took vaccine might think we are safe and no virus can kill us but even though we are vaccinated we are still mortal humans not immortal.

Adjusting to a situation is as hard as losing our ego.

Nature is just a spectator in our lives:

A dog is the King/Queen of their own road or house , it makes sure of nothing happens to the people who takes care of it or residing near it. It is a good listener of what everyone's doing and it is a keen observer of all the things.

A dog doesn't react until and unless some suspicious happens near them , it calls out to other dogs as in unity to bark , because of caution nor a warning sign so to move away.

It takes care of the whole road while they divide and take places by their wish , as the sun rises their job just finishes and they go into their nap but as some sound enters the background. The warrior inside the dog rises up with a sleepy head blinking to see who has become but automatically the mouth starts to fight with it's barking.

A squirrel which is actually a tiny creature but acts very responsible for it's survival as it keeps searching for something but ends up getting nothing .

Just as us humans , we do the same right by telling ourselves there is something even in dead-end.

Squirrel is actually very scared even of the tiny movements of any thing or any person as it runs away far away and comes again to the scene only when it feels safe , we some people in nature are some just as them only right ? Think!

A tree which is withstanding all the pain by the strength of it's roots which is very strongly grounded and it is not moving from one place to another , why also we can't withstand our problems with laying a strong foundation in our lives , and even we have to hold on to only one place/person no matter what the situation is the rainy season, the spring season or the summer.

In between all this how a person who is old in their age reacts when there is a new born baby in their family , they all put their love, priority over it and they find their happiness in them.

Do we humans of all categories always put our love/ happiness on other beings?

Even though how much ever we grow in our professional life , we all go back to a place where we all want to feel vulnerable and get settled in our lives and have children but act as if we really don't want any restriction ? Is it true?

One fine day we will be on our death beds, but today we are sleeping with our blankets on and which is making us cozy , warmer. But tomorrow we don't know if we might or may not end up in dead bed , so all we have is "now" to achieve something small or love or to earn some respect so that there will be no regret for you later on that I didn't give it a try.

Is it that I am pushing you on a negative scale in our lives that we all die and keep fearing when the time comes or either you can think in this way as in there is this extra second, minute, day or a week that we can at least try to do something good and be grateful for every extra time given by the creation of all.

Why we all want to win in our lives , we all want our families only to be safe & happy?

Selfish thinking makes us think that we should somehow just win and that is the definition to a life, I would consider it as a wrong answer because with every failed opportunity there is a new room opening (opportunity) up for you which you haven't still seen , so remember every failed step is a experience to you to reach greater height.

This comes under possessive behavior where no one should talk to our family and create some doubts about them in us , and we say only that we should only win but this whole society is our family which is one called as humans . We are one family not the family with our surname attached to it, but all living humans together without any category filled in with.

Why we always talk to ourselves very silently , because in us there is a defender present inside us who protects us from not reaction to any stupid questions , replies to the person in a way that we don't get hurt mentally and he makes sure he is always protecting ourselves & keeping himself busy over the process of planning of what to do, when to do and how to do.

CHAPTER TWO

Charge

A mobile phone, laptop, tablet anything which requires charge takes efficient time in recharging itself so it can give anything for us in our need , but are we really taking that break such as electronic devices to recharge ourselves and give us a break from everything , no right?

How much ever we keep on charging over 100% it still remains at it , doesn't go over 100 right as 105, 110 but we keep pushing ourselves even over 100% to get to 120 % , that cannot take place at all even though we keep charging.

For example: A mobile which is now at 100% and we take it out from charge for using it , obviously the charge decreases right slowly and comes down to low battery of 10 or 15% before it automatically switches off itself.

Even we should us our thoughts, mind , energy wisely such as a electronic device so that our body shouldn't get stuck in between for over strain .

We should know our strength , weakness and implement in our daily lives so that our body nor mind nor our thoughts switches off automatically.

Recharge ourselves by giving yourselves a break from over stressing your whole body, mind, thoughts.

Don't overheat your brain by even charging over 100%, stay in limits because the phone will burst off one day if you keep charging it over and over again.

CHAPTER THREE

Sacrifice:

Who doesn't sacrifice in their lives everyone does , It's just that we don't show it to people that what we are dealing with it of letting go.

Sacrifices just don't occur like that it requires lot of effort from one to give up on one particular thing or person for a good reason which wouldn't hurt us more in the end of it but the starting part would be very difficult but after taking the baby step never think of returning back to the zero.

One's life is always precious to us whether it comes in the form our wife, girlfriend, husband, boyfriend, daughter, son, father, mother , grandmother or grandfather or our friends or our relatives .

If the other person wants to be left alone let him, sacrifice him and just let it go once and for all rather than pushing him your way of staying in your life is a very selfish thought .

Sacrifices don't come easy we have to give up one thing for having another one in our life just as a mother who has to sacrifice her pain in the time of delivery for her happiness in the form of child , indeed it pains a lot for her obviously and blood also comes out from her but it perhaps make an trademark of her after it grows up , for her blood of it's own she has to give up something right? What we usually do , if we don't get what we want in our life obviously we don't just give up but rather put presser more on the wound ,as a result it will not be healed rather grow into a big wound, so what should we do?

If we want to do something great and achieve something big, well everyone should start sacrificing the comfort zone we are in , as in for example : Let's think there is a small circle and inside there is comfort zone and outside that circle is all about not giving up and fighting it out.

But what we do is get all cozy inside that circle and want to talk to our friends or anyone and gossip about people , we never want to feel sweat and feel the hard work on our bodies so we don't get to bath one more time.

Only if we come outside that circle which you have put by yourselves , you are never going to see a bigger picture which you have been dreaming it all along .

If you want to keep the other person happy in your life then we have to get off from our beds and start working for it rather than wasting time on some non-sense stuff which wouldn't bring anything rather than pain.

So never care about all your loses which you have had till now because all these sacrifices will lead you to a path which is even unknown to yourself , just stay calm , it will automatically lead you to a way which is unexplored.

Everyone has to sacrifice to at least to get something in our lives , we have to sacrifice our sleep in the morning so we burn calories in early morning run, we have to sacrifice at least some thing or some person to reach somewhere in life. But after you succeed in getting what you can, we all can go back to the thing that from now there will be no sacrifices.

Until then keep coming back even though you are being pushed back by yourself.

CHAPTER FOUR

Love

We stride for a better future than now we are in now , for whom?
We strive so the person or people we love could live happily rather than suffer like us, what exactly we end up doing for the sake of love or is it a world where everything is filled up with love perhaps don't know still .
What makes us satisfied until we win something big or achieve some goal that we all desired for but we don't have anyone to share with in our inner circle of our lives .
Do we actually somewhere or the other fall in love with someone or something instantly but we all want to hide it away so it fades just like that keeping a plant without allowing any sunlight to it or pouring in some water in it , so it automatically dries up and die just like our love.
We all feel that we also deserve all the love in the world for good but do we actually care for the person who is actually standing by you and taking a chance every time just to impress you all the time?
We are scared that love can ruin our lives and we might end up in becoming nothing successful ?
But what is success really ? Even if you achieve everything you all ever wished for but with whom are you going to celebrate it and share all your difficulties with

because after you go on to that place , there would be no one with you after all you have climbed up a building ? So who is going to help you but don't think Spiderman would come to rescue!

Our parents takes care of us in the name of love , even though what we do, or we are failing in all our attempts trying still we get that love from them unconditionally , why do they risk so much for love?

Some of us might love more their dear ones, in one sided love story , but is love worth fighting and winning for?

Love is always a team work or in another way you to loose to your loved one and let your team win rather than yourself. Love isn't about giving up , it's all about fighting for !

CHAPTER FIVE

Hatred

We all hate some or the other person in our lives just as we love but for what reason actually we hate them either because they are richer, smarter and well settled than us or is it that we let down ourselves that we cannot overtake them and be successful on day but this will be a more of a competition right between the people we hate and us , actually this can make wonders in our life , so better I call we start hating someone so that at least because of hatred we would reach some destination in our lives .

Basically it was for all the positive people that I said the above lines because they take it as a healthy competition rather than a fight but what for those people who only want revenge in return rather to grow in their individual lives.

Better I would say , this is a very sadistic world in reality or a beautiful world it's in how you take it in and by whom you take in the advice or get influenced with .

Yes , I'm not saying we shouldn't have hatred we should definitely but all that hatred should never used upon a person whom we hate the most , perhaps we should put all that hatred into our works . So all the energy will never go wasted by shouting or thinking/planning on some revenge onto him/her.

So what we should really in our lives ?
Probably it's even like this the most person we hate
would turn out to be the most person we love to be want
to with but in reality and circumstances makes us to hate
them.
If we allow them to hate us, they will or if we allow
ourselves to play our dirty mind around with it will
obviously make our mind messy so what are we going to
deal with it , is in our hands.
Decide wisely what kind of hate do you really want ?
the one which inspires you or expires you from their life?

CHAPTER SIX

Honor

It's time to tell you people what we really for in this existence , I guess you read it right. What and all does honor make us do really which end us up in a tragic result.

So basically a respectful parents who doesn't want their daughter to fall in love with any of the boy because of their honor , so they think that would bring lot of misery to their family name and to themselves but do they think of their daughter feelings or emotions and how much pain it would have made her and turned her heart into a stone by protecting their honor in the society.

We all are bunch of people who want respect at whatever work we do , if we don't get honor where we work at, immediate result will be we quitting from that profession or work .

It all matters to this at last for us all , even the neighbor who stays near our home we expect them to honor with respect but all I want to tell you all who live for honor please don't live false hopes in your living and just waste time because honor can be only achieved or earned by hard work and it doesn't come from the price of money.

They are some incredible people who would kill people because they didn't get proper honor to themselves , are we some godly creature so wherever we go the honor

follows us just like a dog chasing a car .
We all should come to a conclusion from today that we should stop going behind the word honor so we would get a good name in society , but at the end this society would give you nothing in return with this good name .
So look after your life better, but we all want honor right .
Just in case you didn't understand , Cut the chase of receiving honor rather you will get it automatically one day.

CHAPTER SEVEN

Independent

All of us are dependent on either one of the things or one person at least in our lives right now. No matter how many times we think to ourselves that right now in my life I wouldn't want anyone , that point in our lives we would be wanting our lives filled with people but still we feel not connected why because we are still in our world which we have created and carried onto still now.

We are not seeing the bigger picture which is happening in front of us rather than we are focused what might not happen if we don't stand or fight for.

We adopt ourselves to such a situation where even if someone comes us to pull out from a bad situation in our difficult individual lives , we deny and later kind of regret but not fully so we shouldn't hurt ourselves by thinking.

It's all about how we convince ourselves by telling our inner self to just calm down, trust the process for it the queue is long but for the wait is diminishing second by second, minute by minute , day by day , years by years because the longer you keep trying the competition decreases as you will eventually win if only you are being consistent.

Denial is mostly the answer we give because our trust, hope, faith has been broken and that small piece of love which would be left in our soul shouldn't get wasted so we press the button of rejection of helping hands who come into our lives empathizing us even though their profit would be nothing , perhaps their loss will be more .

Alas that we think from sympathy way , this individual is helping from a intention which he is feeling low after seeing in our lowest condition but are we always right from our perspective, perception?

Just think once again why did they react, enact to you like that from their position rather than in receiving end then you wouldn't fight the other person who is coming to lend a helping hand, you will accept it with your two bare naked hands.

If at all you would want to be independent life along I will tell you few examples,

Why are we addicted to social media without that we can save lot of time and be independent right , instead of checking out other's feed we can create our own individual life in reality right.

Why kill so much time by liking, sharing and commenting, I would prefer using all this time by focusing my time on building my profile , portfolio, personal , private relationships . Rather disturbing my mind on what's going on today in the outside world.

Why aren't we focused on building our network zone stronger each day rather arguing over others as the other person has more connections or followers, is that person or someone is stopping you?

You can also build 10 times bigger, better perhaps the best kingdom if only you keep creating, nurturing it every day , life isn't a miracle. It can only be created by working every day not that it comes in one day.

Why can't we also have the best people in our lives helping us out, giving us suggestions, reviews, remarks, their perspective.

If you all want something big in your life , work towards for it, sacrifice, respect yourself for your own decision , never get influenced by anyone because you will be knowing yourself more than anyone.

Don't blindly prioritize people , people change , life makes them get changed according to the situation in their respective life.

In one's life , opportunities cannot be created just like that it takes lot of patience , hard work, trust in your work and the person, to grab it life isn't a idiot to throw it every time . If you fail in your first attempt , go back to basic rules and be consistent, loyal to your goal that you will achieve it .

Later when the second opportunity comes over , don't hesitate by telling the truth because only you know how many sacrifices you have done to get there again, yet again if you are failed, no problem life isn't easy it's all about learning go back to square one begin again but don't repeat the same mistakes which you had done earlier.

We cannot be dependent in our lives too , as my intention would not to tell you be one rather than maintain the balance between the two.

In our lives the people we select shouldn't be toxic, influential, addictive, jealousy, negative.

Rather they should be inspiring, maintain the balance between how to be attached and detached, the one who appreciates our work even if we fail at it, select who accepts us as we are in raw , rather in our social media than in reality.

They say people with a happy face are difficult to find but people with depressive thoughts are very easy to find in many souls.

Why aren't we are up with putting on a happy face because we are not satisfied with what we have in our lives right now rather than we want more in our lives , perhaps we compare with our upper class people , why shouldn't we compare our individual life with the lower class people and convince us that we are living a happy life????

We always are up and running in our lives for we never settle, stop hustling for what we need not worry at all, but at the end we struggle and hustle in our lives whom we don't deserve also but still in the hatred of mind we loose over and convince ourselves that they are required.

Why it's not like we wontedly select the wrong bunch of people in our lives , it's a mere coincidence or it will be a lesson taught by life every time until we learn our mistakes.

CHAPTER EIGHT

Compromise

In some point of life we all let our guard low in front of our loved ones , weakness is love but accepting as they are , we adjusting our lifestyle to their style of living .

All we do in our life will be based on our personal interest rather than we get influenced , it's not like that every time but definitely sometimes.

In our lives we have to accept of what they are offering even if it's little bit with whole heart and soul , it's not like we wanting more from them in terms of expectation to us individual person , they are what will be even if we want to change wouldn't happen . People aren't dolls, robots, to set up the frequency as much we want from their lives, remember one line.

"Expectations always hurt"

In love or in our life , compromise must be there in everyone's life as a important tool , it is used in not losing out people perhaps our guard or value would come down but still the person whom you want the most will be there next to you , in your life journey .

I am not telling you that to lower your guard and make yourselves low, it depends on your perspective.

You will be knowing your loved one's attitude toward their life and the people they treat every time but we wouldn't want to compare with some 3rd person and spoil with what you guys have in between you two.

You be you, never change . Create a trademark for ourselves rather than copying other's lifestyle and getting influential in your life can be overrated and risky for you , because people would always have a graph on you don't keep that changing rather keep it in a same range.

Trust me , it will help you accomplish your biggest goals, achievements with ease.

CHAPTER NINE

Loyal

Being true to a person with your clean heart , without any intentions , throughout your life to a person , dedicating yourself your whole life as you are.

No matter how you are journey is with few people , you still believe , keep faith in them and keep travelling with them even if you find out the pathway in which they are isn't right but the more the merrier , it's not like they would take us to a wrong destination.

Sometimes we have to learn quite few routes in our journey here on this earth , we have to explore all types of roads, mindset of people than only we would know which road, which person will guide us through the rough patch we are going and lead us into a well protected way to a successful life.

If we keep fluctuating from one person to another no one will trust nor keep faith on us, rather we changing our priorities by selecting 1 person for each work , energy will be wasted just like that . Instead being loyal to few people only can cross you the border line which you would be not even going near it.

What will happen if we keep changing our smartphones brand into one another every year, what shall happen if we keep changing our life goals, dreams,

intentions, desires , attraction towards every alternate
person on alternate days?
I don't have an answer for it , it's you who are living
through it , feeling accustomed to the difficulty of situation
not me.
It's you who have to change into different personalities
, become a well trusted person not just anyone in
someone's life .
'Be everyone whom will desire to want anyone'!?
We are human , not machines. We do mistakes by
changing the person whom you love the most and turn
them into your hatred list.
We always hate the people we love , we would enact as
if we like the people we hate.
That's life , my dear friend .
We always tend to cross path in our lives whom we
don't like in our lives.
Life challenges us every day passing by , automatically
makes us disconnected with the people we love the most
by depressing our mind, but we shouldn't get on with it
and convince that nothing has happening , it's just a phase
of life.
The more you understand yourself , more you will be
not deceiving rather be a well sensed being in today's true
nature , perhaps filled with haters, disgusting arrogant
witches , violent monsters, silent gangsters.
The most important ingredient in one's life to achieve
someone or something which is lost to be loyal to that ,
otherwise it would flow like a stream to a place where you
wouldn't even be in the picture.
Just imagine of your would be when there will be no
one standing next to you in your most difficult time ?

But what if you are with a person who has come in your
journey been there since the starting until now?
What would be the difference between the two?
Just think to yourself from your situation and
understand, rather than me telling you more and irritating
your mind and disturb with you a story , make it boring.

CHAPTER TEN

Understanding/ Misunderstanding

In one's life only we can either do two things, one is to understand the other person's explanation of why the person is telling us like that by getting to know the depth of it, but what we do take the meaning in a wrong statement and start showing rage ,grudge onto that person.

Funny right isn't our lives just like the chimpanzee , gorilla in zoo's as they wouldn't know who is coming to look at them . They aren't expecting anything of any kind to be present in front of themselves perhaps they will be themselves just as from before.

The master who makes them understand of how to behave throughout the day and night but how will that master makes them understand is the key , it's not whom we are dealing with .

It's about how we make them understand from their science of language , let it be humans too.

We shouldn't force them on us rather than telling the truth of reality of today's universe , imagining and creating a world for them which fantasy world they are not willing even to listen to it.

The strongest of the warrior never disobey the order from his master by denying that it is not worthy of him to implement in his daily life , lifestyle.

Us humans wouldn't want to be uncomfortable , not get
into any mess, just we are more interested in other's
misunderstanding fights, arguments, wouldn't understand
the situation there and resolve there with peace.
How can we make people understand who are not
ready to listen , only leave the place quietly?
Only one answer is there for us patience and keep
trying ,failing until then keep repeating these three things.
Your goal will be accomplished.

CHAPTER ELEVEN

Opportunities

Life is very easy not that much trouble this colorful paradise will offer to you , it has lot more than very few in everyone's aspect ratio of individual self.

We should make the move not someone would come and give it to us, life is very selfish, selfless, struggle less, strive less, starve less , stride less.

It's about us how we struggle and hustle for each stride for one's personal loved one's we all want right now in our life whom we wouldn't want get very desperate on them but we can be more attention seeking, opportunity craving, attraction wanting, attachment loving.

Life's opportunities would be given to you in the form of eagle's eyesight very sharp , hard to find out, difficult to point at which direction it would be looking out for.

We should grab each , every opportunity which will take us to the highway of problem solving road to our solution of destination.

Every person is important in one's life , all are mere travelers in everyone's journey . Someone is connected to some other person whom you might be not knowing in reality , that' where your life would be better at each point .

It's not like we will choose whom we want in our pathway to go through the flow in our aspect of our lives , but in the same destination more of our friend's friend will be also travelling with you but in different pace and different pathway.

We wouldn't know from whom at what day in our life we would get help by keep pushing our networks more further towards a specified target of goal we would achieve one fine day by trying hard for it regularly consistent on it.

What can we do in our lives if we aren't opportunities grabber?

So be now from now on , don't worry, never get scared of society , people who are talking negative impact on you by consistently trying.

Be happy when you fail , so from that one more opportunity you would have grabbed and you have one more chance to try at least win over the lost battle .

CHAPTER TWELVE

Opinion

We all are different right in our individual lives, it's not like we have the same faces, lifestyle, taste in food, selecting people in our lives, sense of helping and dressing. Some of us different habits in our lives, we keep on changing our sense of giving our own perspective of thoughts who we may or may not influence in our lives who depend on our decisions that they would want to take in each and every step in their personal life.

Our own way of thought process will differ from intentions of a person depending on the people we meet or travel through the journey in the pain of someone's bad behavior or few exempting behavior might hurt us in between by at least standing by them in the side of them of our very own life journey.

There is one saying where people tell you take reviews from many people but at last without getting influential we should decide our own decisions not by taking advices from another or two other but by yourself.

We in our life have certain people whom we only listen to Every time , it's all the time the same person's we go back to when we are very depressed, stressed , or else when want to take a specified decision in our important aspect of our life.

Yes, they are important in our specific individual lives but at every point you comeback after becoming a successful person or after conquering a defeat it's important for us to coming back to you and analyzing what you would want to again face the next time when you go on for the next battle by yourself.
"Everyone cannot teach you everything."
Just like that not everyone can come to you and condolence to you by saying ,it's OK .
Every single time you go out from your comfort zone to achieve something you want that requires lot of potential from within , first comes is your own opinion that is this suitable for you at right amount of time beneficial to us in all types of work or milestone we complete.

CHAPTER THIRTEEN

Suffering

We are just mortal creatures none the less, we get hurt physically, break our bones in accidents , destroy our mental piece of health which would be in peace .
Stress as we take too much from work load , short term achievements which would we put by a chart in our daily cycle in day to day life.
People who beg on streets for penny by penny each for their survival for one meal per day, trans gender's who some forcefully snatch money from us for their survival too, small children who sell pens, few washable car clothes for their living also want to live and thrive through the tough time they are facing.
Some sell eatable things too for to come pass through their life from suffering by surviving from everyday hustle , but what we do usually just pass away from them rather than seeing through their perspective and life, we can at least live our lives to the fullest with full freedom but that small kid which is being carried on the mother hand whom will be taken care of as a adopted kid.
What should so many old aged people should do after they are being thrown out from their own houses , after they are seen begging on the road for coins in the hot sun, where would they sleep everyday, On road they take the

shelter.

One incident happened when I went through the Bangalore road one fine day, A aged women who is around 85 years was seen on a saree which was pretty much filled with only dust , as her skin tone had become quite black as her skin was almost paled out .

She was busy having the food which looked like a packed one, but when she was trying hard to open it as I went near to open it ,she stopped me from opening it and denied me to go near her as she said no one needs to come to help me.

I can manage myself all alone because I don't trust strangers who help me based on sympathy.

I was stunned by her words, literally I could feel her every muscle breaking apart to open that small packed food, later after I asked her what was that she said that her own daughter gave that when she was begging on the road, it we a daily task for her to have food from daughter's hand made food.

No matter how much pain Or suffering we give to our mother she can't be irreplaceable and no one can play that role in everyone's life.

Why you might think that mother wanted to have her daughter's food only from her own hands, because it was her last wish to be fulfilled.

But you guys might again ask about begging, she was thrown out from her very own house for standing against her daughter's husband for not accepting the marriage.

I will leave it here, you can continue the story and end it in whatsoever way you want to end it.

IT'S NOT ABOUT HOW WE THRIVE ,IT'S ALL ABOUT HOW WE VIBE THROUGH EACH OTHER IN ONE'S UNDERSTANDING AT HOME WITH PEACE.

CHAPTER FOURTEEN

Escapism

We all are runners from whom we are scared of the most
from our lives that we expect that might happen in our
lives and us who don't know how to face it with our will
and self confidence.

The ability to defend ourselves after the outcome of the
result which may can go in two ways either in a positive
way or in a negative way through everyone's life up's and
downs.

What we except that leaving we will get everything in
our lives by more people but the person whom we love the
most will be only found to you by yourselves perhaps by
no one.

But what most of us do is keep away them as tagged as
distraction in our lives and keep them away and get
detached from our lives as we press on the button delete
so they wouldn't enter our life again.

Rather than running away from the reality of what
might happen of the end result between you and the other
person we will go to a point in life of where we start
hurting the other person of whom might the best person
in your life , only to eradicate them from our lives.

It's all about participating and not worrying about the
end result because at the end of the day your participation

matters not your result but your personal efforts of how much time we have taken to appreciate the person to explain them how much we would like to take care of them as well as want them in our current life by expressing through our emotions and feelings.

Don't worry , don't hide, face them with your fear of failure , keep trying one day you will find a way to get through the person and win them over.

I can't tell you the ways because each individual has different personality , mindset, way of thinking , understanding, you will be knowing them better than me in and out.

So just go , no problem even though if you have failed some 1000 battles , take all that losing experience which you had faced until now and definitely you will ,must, should win this time.

CHAPTER FIFTEEN

Trust

Have you ever heard about instinct , mindset about
yourself , gut feeling.
Whenever your these three tell something it well be
the truth about your feeling , never or ever it will go wrong
or prove that you have made a mistake in your life by
trusting them.
Whatsoever this world might tell you that you are nuts ,
seems he has gone crazy in his life now by trusting them
but when we might go wrong is after to start listening
people's speech about life of how people are getting settled
in their personal life.
Remember this you are special, you have some talent
that you have not explored that side, trust that you change
the world by taking over just as the storm.
Why can't you, just question yourselves ?
It's just away from a single step we take in our lives.
For starting a marathon we should first take a proper
base of foundation then only we can start off the lead
earlier otherwise we would be left behind just like that
without nothing.
For us to Participate in the marathon , we need some
support from the fans too considered as friends who can
help us by pushing us that extra mile just as the music does

in the gym while working out.
In the end we would want someone to help us out in the middle of nowhere from their help we will achieve the goal we badly want since from our childhood.
Have faith on yourself that you will definitely will win this battle of forgiveness, sacrifices, love, all going through the air.
If we have the right intention to fight away the negative spirit in us , we should never let that consume us and win over us.
We should only focus on the main target, goal which we would have targeted in the long run in our life.

CHAPTER SIXTEEN

Settled

Who are well settled in their lives, nothing is for permanent and forever just stays for short period of time .
We just think from our perspective that their life is well settled , as they are living their life independently but their life stress, personal goals, achievements , milestones that inner peace of life which most of them don't have in our daily life will we go on to think other things which are not Important to us, which fetches us nothing to our life.
The energy will be wasted by putting our mind into someone's life , rather that time can be focused on ourselves to improve us as individuals. More Energy, time, focus would be saved and invested on us only as being selfish , doesn't matter to us if we are selfish at last we are successful or not that matters to the society.
People who are not settled will be still searching for a right path to get settled down in their personal life but no one will be there to guide them through the rough patch but we should stand up for ourselves because no one will, as known everyone is busy in their own life problems and worry .
Nobody cares about you , no one is waiting for you to get settled, nor they are interested in your struggling story , the whole world wants to see, listen to the successful and

well settled stories.
Fail so much that every time you comeback fighting just remember how you went down losing, never repeat the mistakes which you have done earlier so you're time, energy will be saved.
Know your enemy which is you, remember it's always you vs. you.
How You convince yourself to get up each and every time after losing badly, no problem losing is a learning process where you will learn more and explore more about you which is always good.
Don't worry your time will come, I would rephrase it as we should only make the time come near us rather than waiting for the right time do it now, do it wrong, do it again with better off yourself.

CHAPTER SEVENTEEN

Life

1) What do u make out from this so called Life!!?
2) What is life?
3) What did life give u?
4) What did u give to your life?
Well my answer to my first (1) question is.... As follows below!!!
Well what is life :) -
Life I define like this, we will be born from mother womb, come out of the mother's womb and we will be know nothing about this world leaving our mom and dad :) -, obviously relatives also. As we keep growing from 1 month to 2 to 3 months fast forward 1 year, 2 years we start to speak, think a little, walk a little, run a little, I will remind u still we think in that age that our family is our world and we will not be having friends will come back to this point later, then we grow to 4 years, 5 then our parents push us to school obviously we have to and come the word friends ;) -,') where we will not be knowing what kind of a relationship that will be and we start trusting them more than our parents, we start telling our secrets only to our friends rather than telling to our parents. Who are these friends, what are they, what do they do with our lives, will tell u what happened with me,

Friends are the ones who protect us, help us in giving suggestions how to propose a girl /boy, and will be there in time to back us, not all and not everyone **.

Friends are like just outsiders, they have to be met wren you are going to school, college, outing, movies is made up for friends like so time pass, they aren't coming in our daily lives, they just can't, it cannot happen, it's the reality.

Well still I didn't answer my 1st question right here it goes,

Life just goes on without u or with u on this earth, we can just work hard and expect a good result from life but if u don't get a good result, just don't run away from this world who is speaking against u, face those bad people with anger, never run away from this society who is talking dirty to u or to your family just control it don't talk back, hold your tongue back and work, work, put in the hard work it pays off, don't ever listen to those dogs who are shouting against just maintain your class and keep your standard high always don't go to their standards and fight with them.

No one will come to help you out in this life leaving your parents, own family, and your girlfriend might help u if u have :) - no I'm single!!!.

So just keep those friends away as much far as u can I am not saying u to push them, just don't keep them like your family.

My (3)answer

Life gave me so much opportunities but I ran away.

Read down please :)

I just ran away from this opportunities because I couldn't face these people who were talking bad about me, and I couldn't face them and there were no one to support me, no friends, no support came from my girlfriend kind of she is my ex now but she isn't a girlfriend actually.

I couldn't just hold on to that pain alone, so ran away from that opportunity. Couldn't face this world alone.

My 4th answer

Well I can say after I ran away I came back strong, stronger, I was the strongest to fight against this world all alone, but couldn't win the battle, yes I gave my everything to win it but I won over myself now I can fight any battle in the life all alone, I can listen to anyone who talk shit to me I don't care now because I have my two good friends in my life, well I can say they aren't my friends they are much more than my family and now I can withstand the storm, all alone.

Thank you:) -

CHAPTER EIGHTEEN

Loneliness

Whomever we love the most in our lives, hurt us the most and leave us and go and will never comeback into our lives and teach us a lesson and go that don't trust anyone.

One very small example I want to give you guys,

One boy called saran was there in his childhood, he had a friend called Keshawn and he was only dependent only on him. Like they both were in football so this saran was only dependent on Keshawn and was not talking to anyone and saran wanted Keshawn as attacker next to him so that he can score a goal with help of him.

Everything was going on well (practice) , one fine day a tournament was announced so saran was named captain and he named Keshawn as vice-captain.

Actually Keshawn was more effective as a footballer than saran but saran had influence so he had to be captain and saran was only depending on Keshawn all the time even in defense and even in scoring goals.

So, with help of Keshawn saran also played well and they won that tournament. They got admitted to the same school because this saran forced Keshawn to join with him because he could not live without him as he was that much dependent on him.

Later one day, Keshawn got into a very bad fight and he had to change the area and go to a different place and this friendship had to come to a end and these two golden friends got separated and they couldn't meet for at least 5 years.

This saran got to know the real world that time when Keshawn left him and went to a different place, so this time saran got maturity and became very independent from that time.

But later in saran life whomever he met had to go very far from him and he was all alone, didn't have people to share his feelings, pain, emotions.

Later he got to know that the people who give love the most to their loved ones, God removes that loved ones from our lives and gives us a person whom we don't even like them and tells us get adjusted with them whom you don't like and learn.

Loneliness comes to us when people don't react to us or respond, and let us not take a wrong step in our life, let's tell our loved ones what's happening in our mind rather than us thinking that what will they think if we tell we are struggling from loneliness.

I am making this topic because this is a reminder for all of us, let's not ignore anyone anymore, even if we are busy message them back, that you are busy, even think from their point of view.

It's been a month and a day, and he still will be remembered and loved by me until I die and my soul will be searching for the right answer, why what made him do like that.

Let's reach out to our closed ones /loved ones and take care of them instead of giving our mind to ego, why should I call him /her, let's only first teach out and be in touch

with everyone.
If we find time to reach out people and for helping out people in their difficult times, this will do good for us when we are in difficult situations.
So let's get on to helping people who are in need of helping hand.

CHAPTER NINETEEN

Dreams

Including me everyone wants to get fulfilled their dream by getting there , for every individual person it will be different in their lives to live their fullest.

In everyone's life someone or another will be there who wants us to achieve something in our life, somewhere down the line we would be having more people enacting as nice but will be hoping that we wouldn't want to come up in our life.

I had a dream of writing a blog first before writing my book, later once after I starting blogs my views started to rise , later my second dream was to publish my book on Amazon ,Flip kart and Kindle e book.

I extended my dream to write 3 books which was published on all commerce websites , now I have written over 30 blogs and this is my 4th book.

If I had not dreamt of this I wouldn't have shared so many interesting stories with you my lovely people, it's me who kept fighting against me that I want the world to read stories which are as a mirror to the nature true self.

Whatsoever I had dreamt of becoming until now , out of 90% I have at least gotten into 80% because that much I was focused into it, remaining 10% was out of my mind so I don't mind.

I was thinking of what explanation should I give in this topic, later I realized why shouldn't it be myself because it's copyright free.

Keep dreaming big so you will come to point where you will Follow them only because all days if you are focus is on only one than the graph of your life will go up like a straight line.

If we don't know what we want from our life , we should get adjusted to the situation of we wouldn't want to be which is very uncomfortable to live with.

Life's too short to experiment with rather be confident on your dreams , follow them today, now.

Tomorrow the world will follow the same path which was created by your dream.

CHAPTER TWENTY

Nullity

Without you in our life what will be left to us in our lives ,
it will be only I means only yourself (absurdity).
When in pain we feel nullity means emptiness in one's
individual life just as the trees without leaves in it, without
water as in proper nutrition to them to live in this
existence.
Are we some celebrities in our lives no right , even we
are common men who are living along us , so we have to
wait for everyone to come into our lives specifically ,
individually later have to filter one by one into only a few
who can provide us mortal help, mental strength , physical
appearance to make us smile.
When not having anything in our lives we will be more
with freedom of taking decisions because we will be not
having much options, or more positions to fill into it.
Self-doubt if we have on ourselves then, one should
approach some friend to help his/her problem out because
emptiness leads to blankness which later will end up us in
a dark room where we would find difficult to find the light
, perhaps we would prefer more dark rather than finding
light. The trust on light will be gone forever and better
change yourself or take help from someone who you listen
to.

Life is very precious not blank , nor depressing to sit alone and keep thinking about the blunt mistakes which we had done in the past .
Wait for your right turn , keep working for it until you find peace in the light, there lies the success of your return from dark.

Silence prevails

Work hard dedicating your every energy into it, the results will do the talking as they say it is the universal truth which will make you do things out of your reach from your comfortable zone, by making you out of reach for your next destination , until it reaches your own personal goal.
Rather than we speaking for ourselves and looking bad in front of the society, giving your work , first priority , doing it consistently each and every time .'
The success of your work will gradually grow because the more you get on the level they would want to come into your existence and make fun of you and tell you unwanted things , just tell only one thing to yourself that you have not heard anything , I don't know anything and who are they first of all to decide what to do in our lives.
Time will give answer to everything which ever aspect of life we would want to achieve in our lives.
Never react to the people who tell negative things to you or who give negative vibes, just smile I promise you will feel better.
Never enact to be someone whom you never are , don't imitate people because you already have an identity in this world try to work on yourself , build your profile and make some good network so that will be there for lifelong beside

you.
Just smile and stay silent that's your answer to any
rumor coming your way.

Reality

How's the world as in today , or how it will be tomorrow you will be knowing how it can be transformed day to day life in different types of age group , categories of mindset where we decide how to be applicable in between the people who can actually be helpful to change this universe concept of changing some set of person's mindset from day dreaming to be in their specific island of comfort zone into hard working reality ,while this could be a complete changeover for them who would never want to struggle and keep their place in uprising today's world as in society.

Some have accustomed relations of toxic towards their habits of letting go from their sacred ones to empower youngsters whom will want to transform next generations of coming tomorrow,

Few are focused on their own targeted goals, dreams which they will want to achieve it, should do because of their commitment towards lifetime satisfaction would only come after getting to that aimed point in their souled mind.

Many would want just go with the flow as they would having some ambition in life to become but their current situation in their present life due to the ongoing trouble which they would want to somehow come across it ,

perhaps even after coming through .
Many more problems which will be impossible to fight
with their bare hands , it shall to trouble them throughout
their lives just as their fate which will be just out of the
sight to get settled and run across.

CHAPTER TWENTY-THREE

Power

Voice of voiceless people to become powerful without
being Powerless.
Power is what we have in our hands, as it can be
compared to remote.
Almost everyone have a remote in their houses,
As even we have individual voice,
Everyone wants power in their hands,
As remote in their hands,
Power in their minds,
Everyone wants power in their hands,
Everyone wants to raise their own voice,
and create some noise,
They want to be heard through their perspectives,
By their channels of interest by television,
They wouldn't be nerd to sit idle,
We will be forced , suggested to see their of channels,
rather giving us the opportunity,
to Speak by putting up our own channel,
Perhaps all may get a chance to change channel or may
not get to
raise their voice,
Alas, shall I give up, should I wait, will I create a chance
by myself,

No, I shall make sure my voice reaches every audience,
Through my own channel,
We must be heard everywhere,
To people, politicians, even though we are not heard for
now,
Because we are being influenced by other perspectives/
channels,
Get on with your own channel and make them hear,
make them hear, get them near,
they will be here.

CHAPTER TWENTY-FOUR

Friendship

It takes years of togetherness in the form trust , faith, lots of secrets to be kept and shared , as well as few promises we make to them so that we can be accountable in our lives to achieve our self-goals which we would have kept as token promise to yourself to satisfy our short need in many worlds but transferred as one artificial world turned into an automobile garage life for us in whole.

A friend's ear is the safest place to tell all our secrets, tell all our regrets which we have done until now , getting ideas for our personal relationships , how to get along in our toxic lives in daily life.

Who doesn't love their friends , they play a vital role in deciding our important decisions . They are the one's whom we almost everything which happens in our daily life , immediately also mention them if something goes wrong in our lives in the first place.

If we are feeling low we call them, message them or meet them to surpass our sadness, it really feels refreshing after talking to our buddies and telling almost all our gossips, funny incidents, angry accidents with annoying people .

It really takes lot of sacrifice even from their side like giving us confidence : when we are put down , gaining us

strength : when we are weak , spending time with us :
when we need them the most.
Friends doesn't mean that they have to meet you in
person and support you with physical presence, even
though they can't meet you in reality their presence would
be felt through their actions of words by their nature.
It's not mandatory that you would get all types of
friend's in one category but you will only find the rarest
friend only through the weirdest way in your journey of
your life in an unexpected , undesired way most probably.
I would like to share one small example in my life;
In my life even though I have not seen my friend (a
close one) but wouldn't like to mention whom , they are
very close to me in my life right now from almost a year.
Even though we don't talk everyday , it's like we cover
the life portions of problems which happen between us in
one call away rather than meeting in person.
They are equally important in my life as everyone as
but it's not like they have separate priority over all, but
their essence in my life is very essential.
They have not met me physically but they make me feel
they are mentally present with me all the time .
I'm with them. They want my help , motivation, if they
are going through some mental health issues I would be
there for them throughout.
So all I want to say is meeting a person in reality
doesn't really affect or make a person good, their true
nature, value for time to be given for us matters a lot, how
consistent they will be without changing in a loyal way.
Some friends only stay as a friend to you on your social
media, just as they want to show to their friends and be
accountable and put on the mark list in the cart. They
wouldn't talk to us frequently or we wouldn't most often ,

it's just that they are present in our life and be absent from
our life journey completely.

• 93 •

CHAPTER TWENTY-FIVE

Family

What life is without loving and caring people filled in with home as along through our ups and downs in our journey love filled destination throughout in and out.

People who don't have anyone to share their feelings with whom they share the blood with is like fighting each other and not letting down too.

Us in a family who don't fight as if we are killing each other with perspectives filled with lots of expectations , love, over caring nature , still if what will you earn in our lives if we wouldn't have someone of our own from our bloodline who knows what not until our life might end but still what can we do rather than love each other over fighting.

Without a fight in a family there doesn't cook food , it's like people who fight more together have more bonding , have more feelings so it doesn't need us to quarrel like we are enemies but shall remain as always and forever.

There's compromise in life along with whom we share our lives everyday , sacrifices we make to just reach the outcome of the utmost and uprising with the limitations of our relatives as well as for our cousins . Including our grandparents who understand our concern , requirements make a lot of efforts to convince us indeed will help us to achieve the long term ambitions which can conquer our worlds.

Life would not be as easy as expected according to our limitations, worry, troubles, difficulties which will definitely come across in everyone's lives just as equal to each and everyone with many of them would not be easy for only an individual to right of difference by each other differentially but in different aspects of life.

It's like travelling together in a bus through a specified destination journey which would be like taking along everyone's problems , difficulties , understanding each other and compromising in each other's lives just for the good for others life so that the family tree glooms around and gives shadow for the whole family and live peacefully.

CHAPTER TWENTY-SIX

Voice of Voicelessness

Each and everyone in their life would be voiceless at least in some point of their individual life.

Life will throw a situation where our situation would be only watching how the world travels through rather than going in between and change the people who are voiceless right now throughout their life would be the same without any change as constant.

As people struggle for lack of consistency in their specific lack of confidence , self- trust , trusting your intention right with your gut feeling.

The lack of backing our only interest in the field through our most loved thing to do in our lives but what we do on the opposite side of what we like or what we get more forced to get from our families but where would be the self satisfaction for his soul?

Even though we are voiceless in our lives such as in our settled life, we would want to achieve something out of the world , as wouldn't want to conspire many things to do on our watch list to clear off all your self-established goals.

Who would speak for us if we wouldn't speak for ourselves to show the world what you are made of more better than what people expect out of you, we wouldn't want to fall out from the daily path of hustle while we would go for the achievement.

We are all beggars in our lives , we also beg just as beggars who would plead for being guilty, asking for peace, wanting to be loved or to love the other person.

We are not satisfied with whatever we have right now in our lives , as we would want to be more just asking for more food on our plate rather than having the food with what we get served in our plate and having it.

What are we rather than a beggar who is asking for money on the road every time, everyday for the same money without any greed but what he is doing will go for his food and lifestyle more than the saving he can't do from it to go as in from that to bank and deposit it.

What we do is the total opposite of that. Rather than accepting what we have, we would want to gain more , keep raising from all the above in our lives and defeat everyone in the competition.

It's not like we all want to gain more fame than money but would want both currently as an individual to live for respect and live a life with fullest of more modesty , artificial social fake life than a happy independent private low-key life without any tensions and worry.

Life would be more peaceful if we can start living for ourselves rather than to impress others , by adjusting our happiness to gain their attention, mass audience through the rough patch of our lives keeping at risk by entering the zone which we are not even into.

Keep it simple , easy to achieve.

CHAPTER TWENTY-SEVEN

Perspective, Priorities, Preferences, Possibilities , Probabilities, People

We all are humans, so we become weak, selfish, jealous, do
Sacrifices, at last, we are just "mortal fools" who can get
hurt physically and mentally, die at any time either by
Natural cause or in an accidental way,
It's just all about "perspectives of the way we think and
we receive it"
It all comes under one perspective if you think from
your end, we can only feel why we were told or received in
a different way only when we think from their
perspective,
Probabilities of chances we could get or have either in
past or in future,
Possibilities of the events which can turn around any
second or movement,
Problems either we will be having or would get in
future,

Everyone will have problems or will face them but it depends on how we solve it,
People of whom we select in our lives,
It all comes down to whom we are with either with positive people or negative people, the influence will come through them only,
Priorities we give importance to people over our personal choices should be taken in an individual way,
Probabilities while we take few important decisions in our lives carefully as we think down to cut less contact between the people who create ruckus among people amongst us with the longing way as we go through along the journey.
We don't get to choose problems on our own, even people, in that case, have the same outcome when we go through some difficulty but it's how we work through those tiny gaps in between our lives and face it to reach a specific individual peak in our personal life.
The more crowded we get along in mindset of few person's lives, lesser amount of freedom , more pressure of influence we will be taking in from them and implementing , experimenting to see what can happen to our goals, achievements as we pass out the targeted milestone.
People don't stand with what was, or is , it's more they stand in peace and watch out for the drama which may take place in their environment and will be very excited to share it with their friends, relatives and share it on their social media.
Instead if they had helped people who are fighting out in the public through many differences such as change in way of thinking, compromising and accepting as they are.

There would be only silence, peace and happiness around the whole society , world.

CHAPTER TWENTY-EIGHT

Memories

What would life be without all the sweet moments we intake through without any proof of our devices , how it could be for us to live in this existence to live with these many toxic people who would only ask for more in life.

It doesn't take much time for us to make whole lot of efforts to impress one being who are close to us by making it recorded and show it to all the people whom we travel across in our journey but what it would be for us if the other person isn't present in that situation in your personal life to be physically for experimenting with different aspects of emotions which we go through daily.

They say memories can't be created but shall be dreamt of having one in our specific lives individually rather what would happen if it doesn't happen according to the plan which we had thought of, the whole dream would be demolished into broken pieces.

It's like how we travel each day in this universe , down the memory lane as we keep travelling down the experience which we would have faced long back in that period of time would sound funny now after remembering it and sharing that incident with our family and friends.

Our time just flows as fast as stream but as it keeps flowing our life runs through it with the competition of others in it by the time we reach a specific age where we would fed up of strangling between these bunch of unmatured people with less amount of energy left within us , as we take rest like stream reaches a ocean or bay of Bengal .

Just like us after coming to one certain of age where we would rest completely and look back at all the mischiefs, lot of drama, many of love stories would be rusting through our mind , very few of good deeds which would be done in that span of our lives, daily fights of us with our parents would hit us back when our children start fighting against us.

It's like we are plotting some sort of plan against our grandparents but what will happen is our own children will be aware of our whole mindset of how we will be reacting to them instead of us to our parents.

Life's very short to spend time thinking about all lost souls, relationships which we lost in the battle of self-respect, love, heartbreaks.

It's up to us how we manage everything mixed with a full pack of emotions, feelings, pain, extravagance , disbelief over us, respect towards whole bunch of living species who wouldn't want to spend rest of all eternity with all the pain, emergency which can cause the change in the process towards our effort to change the mindset of people.

Whereas, it's easy for us to choose what kind/ type of memory we would want in our life as a permanent to be present even while we take our last breath.

Our mind acts as the permanent google photos which doesn't require any temporary backup over Wi-Fi , for storing our most important memorable photos taken over the moon of our love life in this universe , most importantly it doesn't get deleted even if we try to delete it temporarily from our mindset.

Life is very unpredictable sometimes even it feels scary to lose out on many opportunities we might miss out while we carry out some important plantations with some very clueless decisions with all our hopes, desires , dreams ,ambitions, faith on a specific person but after getting to know the real person after spending some time with them through different aspects of memories we would get to know the real shade of the person, later what can we decide up to in our lives to keep them or to exit from their lifetime so that experience , experiment which we undertook from a long time would go into waste.
Perhaps all that energy which has gone waste can be at least saved from now on by silently backing up yourself from that toxic relationship or by respecting yourself and stop talking to that person.
At the end of the day , it's our wish to how we want to spend all our lives , either by taking all the best of the memories and watching it in the bed or regretting what we have done by making wrong decisions.
Keep it simple, and achieve what you have come into this existence.
Be consistent in what you are doing , definitely the victory will be yours one fine day until then more people will be denying you the end result but when you reach the end line of your victory , later will come to ask your success journey way through of how it was thoroughly.
Remember and mark out the people to tell your success story to all of them who are not responding for your help ,

later on your hard work will make them bring it in to you.

CHAPTER TWENTY-NINE

Acceptance

Of many creatures in this universe who would you want to go down to their level and let through them in your life , go ahead decide yourselves with your own mindset from your own very decisions but be very careful in selecting them and putting it in your highlighted list of closed ones, but the more close to you they are more treated as enemy to you rather as a friend.

It's all about choice you make of selecting the right person whom by making them a permanent member in your soul, mind, personally, physically with all your heart but what shall happen if you choose the wrong person with a rightful set of mind with enacting skills, how would you go through your existence with a devil by your side of walking alongside with every aspect of your lives , what can be done without doing it really in - person with whole intention to getting with their intentions right.

If we select an equal amount of time for all the types of hype we give importance with divided time for all kinds of species in our living , then only the true nature of a being can be only understood by us in the timeline.

How can we select the right people in our lives and accept them as the right set of persons in our lives? We as individuals like different types of attitudes, thinking , and mindset in people so the choice can be personal.

Only one thing can be said is , we can select any kind of we like or love but to go through some milestone , by achieving and making it a success story we need a person who inspires us, influences only to do right things in specific amount of time , the one who stands by us every time and fights against the demon who is opposing us to do the right thing.

So, let's get on to selecting people who do more than the above people , sacrificing their dreams and fulfilling our ambitions and turning both of our desires into reality.

Who doesn't want to win big in our lives , but for all that build up what should we do , how many lessons it might take to achieve it , how much losses we would be facing, lots of opposes which we will take in, our patience will be tested again and again every time, are we loyal towards the specified target which we are focusing on, too many distractions will come in our way to disturb our main goal .

The main aspect in our life should be to never let go of the most loved thing we want in our lives, no matter how long it might take to get to us. Keep trying, pushing until your faith leaps into a full fledged tree from a sampling.

CHAPTER THIRTY

Sympathy/empathy

Seeing people through kindness, showing mercy and donating something with what we have right in our hands is sympathy.

Thinking from their perspective , getting emphasized for all their efforts , hard work , struggle which wouldn't have taken place without any help is considered as empathy.

People are still confused between the two words , just wanting to tell the difference between the two .

What can be changed in today's society , nothing more than the style of thinking of how we can transform people from one place to another where it can generate more number of rightful people who can take decisions independently by their own influence without any sympathy or empathy within their lives can change their whole setup of living.

We get very emotionally attached to people who wouldn't have anything in their lives ,by telling ourselves why God makes them like that (sympathy). We don't stop it there , rather tell it to more sets of person's where we would be hurting their mindset and feelings too.

That makes us think why shouldn't we give something as a donation so their life would be simpler than by at least

them struggling for food , shelter and proper materialistic things in life.(empathy)
What change can we make from our daily lifestyle so our whole set of person's who are facing problem in deciding what to do with their sympathy / empathy mindset, it's very easy for an individual to decide upon a decision just by being accountable to your friends or to your cousins who can understands your whole concept of mindset and thinking in wholesome throughout your life.
Why cannot we take the decisions independently ,obviously we can definitely can go through them individually not just by talking to ourselves.
But by taking the responsibility on our own shoulders , we can be accountable just to be ourselves by telling our inner-self person to stand by whatever decision you are taking for the welfare of the society.
It's not easy for a single person to take a leap into a whole new universe which he/she might not be experienced to make wholesome decisions just to clarify his thoughts and justifications towards a single product/ person.

CHAPTER THIRTY-ONE

Express/impress:

The right amount of expressions we give to an object when we are overjoyed with a lot of excitement with a lot of joy , out of the world with lots of expectations over it .

The amount of time, energy , efforts , sacrifices , compromises , struggle we put in to just get the shadow of their smile in our ocean of our lives with majority of hopes, faith and trust as we put in the leap of pain away which we would facing in the society , even criticism doesn't come into our existence when we decide to go to the other mile , for getting that extra pound of happiness to satisfy our life's utmost goal.

It's not at all about how we get dressed up , put our facial mask on, putting our best on perfumes just to express our feelings, emotions just for the sake of happiness which we would get for the sake of satisfactions which we would get in the end of the day while we travel all along the days where we would be travelling with it all along.

How we feel about a person should be only told from their actions , along with that should be expressed in the form so that it shouldn't be a ruckus for anyone who is passing by us , it doesn't matter how your attire is , how is your lifestyle, how many artificial devices you have, how many cars you have.

It all comes down to only how you would take care of the person even without money in the existence by putting all your love, how much you can sacrifice people just to get to the end point of a destination through a journey in a winning way, it's all alike how you create your bonding with the other person , understanding them through their ups and downs , even though you aren't on the talking terms with the other person .
You should be knowing the person in and out , love is not all about giving up but fighting for both of them even though the other person has given up, it's your responsibility to realize how your bonding was the best and not jumping into any conclusion by not letting go of that weirdo.
The merrier 10 beautiful moments you have , perhaps over 1 bad movement which has destroyed your whole relationship, but how you are going to try to console the other person and winning them and get settled in your life will be a big challenge for you in this whole corrupted , criticized world where love has no more value in today's world.
Fight for what you want, Light for what isn't dark , Almighty may work in your favor.
Magic is there in love, miracles can happen over consistency.

System

How's our ecosystem behaving in today's life depends upon how we react in the opposite side of our behavior in spite of difference in opinion.

Life's not getting easy for the lazy people who aren't really focused in real life scrutiny by today's competition over the people lives is being targeted by soft sided behavior , it's not at all worthy for fighting which is not in our hands is what the young generation is thinking but the technology is taking it's own way into the future by taking storm over the internet.

The world as in today as transformed totally turned it's head on to the nature by creating, evolving into a whole new digital world .

But it's not like we are expecting more from the digital world , it is the competition in today's world that has made the global leaders to run through in every part of the world for the right product , atmosphere right now is demanding more supply of business 2 consumers retail market.

Education system has to be changed more into a developed nations as in where the knowledge should be used as power , perhaps not converting the education system into commercial brands , advertisements and totally into only business schemes.

Indians should not only support healthy environment on the education systems, clean slate politics, neat and corrupt free government but also should provide equity of rights to decide the decisions which is taken by the government in order to have our thoughts, perspectives, ideas into implementing it.

It's not every time about bribing people , looting poor people's money .

Influence is being used as an important tool wherever we go in our lives, without that we have been treated as a nomad, it's like a important tool to have with us wherever we go.

When will the common middle man find his peace by not roaming , by not bribing higher class people , when will we go to places without heavy heart and a unworried mind , with a peace of mind.

It's time to change , for us to elect corrupt free leaders , to see a change in politics and welcome new young generation to lead us.

Let's be united and fight for what we would get , not being greedy for more. Go on youth , be spiritual, challenging , questionable to the leaders , to the ones who are trying to play with the system.

CHAPTER THIRTY-THREE

Hope

Hope is a very good thing to hold on to believe that good things will happen to you in a strong way, otherwise there wouldn't be no potential for one to live on this planet for existence nor the excitement to go through and enjoy the pain with our hearts filled with pain, joy, expectations , sorrow.

Hope isn't a dangerous thing to strive , if one wouldn't able to move along with hope will give up in their young age.

Life throws too many acquisitions , distractions to divert us from the biggest hope which we ever would be fighting in ourselves over the victory of the lost of too many defeats which would be more depressing , disappointing, disrespectful for us in our specific lives.

It isn't easy for a king to keep losing in the battles which he would be knowing of his defeats but sometimes he must think what he should take on to the next battle , you might all say hope .

Nope, he should gather all his men , women give them courage and tell them that we should show it to the universe what we are made up of, even though from years we are been struggling for one small piece of victory over our consistency which is lacking, self - discipline, being loyal with unity of freedom to fight for the lost love of hope in our lives must be regained today by our free will to fight come what may.

Just imagine what would happen if we all go through some difficult phase in our lives , what would be our first reaction is to give up.

If that only can be changed by not expecting a victory rather than hoping something good might happen , perhaps it's better than thinking negatively.

I'm not so sure about everyone's confidence towards of a specified dream project which might be written down years back and be achieved over years of togetherness, dreaming of becoming successful in it and will complete that milestone with whatever time remaining in our spam of our lives individually.

Hope cannot destroy one's dream but re-generate the people's ambitions in their lives by bringing prosperity , some positive vibes into the nature of human brain, might stop us from over thinking to achieve our goals.

It's just like the oxygen we breathe , more hopes we have to be dreamt and desired of , the more we will have freedom of options to select with the right amount of energy to be used.

Just keep trying your luck by pushing your efforts bar high by taking your game next level in your life by hoping your successive projects as examples and keep moving forward until the destination is arrived, later after you reached hope for everyone's health.

CHAPTER THIRTY-FOUR

Rage/Revenge

Having grudge on some people , things will cost you more rather than gain you nothing mere than 1 second satisfaction , later it would be turned into a regret after you realize what have you done.

Taking severe action on the person, thing which has caused you some unforgettable incident in your life will only make you land in jail or in the court, it's not like the other person wontedly committed that trouble on to you, unless it was a supari.

We cannot measure same as all the people who live out there in today's world , you have to maintain your own value which shouldn't be diminishing at all, rather increasing nor be constant in either way.

Life plays lot of dice games between you and many people whom to choose, what shall be required to do in the right place as according to their right time will be decided by fate , by the person whom you may have some disbelief over you or someone related to you.

It isn't always revenge or rage takes the victory in people's life, it will cause more either blood loss, relationship loss between people, misunderstanding takes over , too many troubles such as roaming in and out of police station and court.

What can be the victory give us to the world over fighting world as in today?
Compromise , understanding the under statement of each and every person involved in that specific case according to the equal of problems should be calculated , divided into certain groups of persons of how should we react to it in a silent way with peace offering ,so the quarrel will stop between many.
It's not about who wins or who loses , it's about who conquers the truth in the real world of reality by their true nature.
World as in today doesn't really learn on people's mistakes more than the errors of human which is caused by the greediness of money, fame and power.

patience, planning, execution:

Maintaining calm under every circumstance , facing silence even while the truth wins over the evil of fake social dilemma.

Time is the real winner of all , over the drama of everlasting period drama by selfless people over selfish needs over the people for taking over their competitor in the race.

Life may dump you down even while running into your long time running project may erase you from existence , but it will show you a way if you are only loyal to your existence and living by maintaining a single life attached to your main intention by not revealing it , perhaps you can be accountable but only to a few.

Patience is like having permanent tool in your life , even while you are running out of every aspect in your life.

The only option for lone victory shall be first patience.

Planning is mere just how essentially you can think of a

person who can be helpful throughout your difficult situations while you simply walk away from the route which you had marked it way before anyone, but this one can actually make your pathway smooth by enabling the formula by getting you to the easiest of ways to pass through the seven oceans and reach your life.

Obstacles may come many but you sticking on to the fair amount of time, sheer planning towards a directory target may go on until and unless you are completely sticking on to your plan.

Have only one plan , if plan a fails , have a plan b: that would be backing your only plan a. Never change your plans rather make few adjustments to that and continue to pursue it will guide you to the never seen victory.

Execution is more important rather than planning, you shall have whatever plan in this world but how you are going to convince yourself and others who would help you through to take down the plan to execute it to fulfill it with your whole heavy heart , even though it might be something very new to you but the main intention would be not coming out of the plan to not give up on your final step to achieve your ambition.

Fight it out , it's only you who can convince 1000s of people by just believing in your true self , in your ability , if you can make a strong will you will and can make your plan a successful one.

CHAPTER THIRTY-SIX

Greed/selfish/jealous

us

Wanting more in life as per you would be having more than enough in your lives but still you convince yourself that only a little more i want just like that , little more will be transferred into more and more , keeps growing like a tree.

Not want to help others, first you want to be settled rather than others how are to be in their lives you wouldn't want to care about without any hesitation and any haste .

People who would want to make more name , money , fame would require some sort of self - sorted goals , getting irritated by those we can't afford to be .

Perhaps we would want only us to be everything that there can be in this existence , rather what we don't understand is that this world is for everyone who is there in this hugely vast population , but what can we make of these selfish thoughts which can be easily distributed over to anyone.

We would not want to explore more in this life rather than want everyone to hear out all our words, thoughts, to be influenced by our actions, so that we will get the best out of today's technology which is remaining over only for us.

Freedom

The speech of rights to everyone has been given after we got independence by the freedom fighters , but still why are we caged inside like an escaping bird who wants to fly away into the world and live up to its potential by taking its own decisions , solving problems by itself .

Few wouldn't want to take risk by going out of the boundaries which they have put to themselves in their individual lives by establishing few trademarks by natural impact which they would get in the society while facing some criticism from the people we know especially hurts more not to spread our own wings to fly by believing perhaps what we do is forget that we can take a long jump and start flying in the empty sky which is filled with opportunities of grabbing it.

Life isn't very complicated as expected. We think it is very complex but we think it is compound.

If it isn't our way of selecting the right set of opportunities with our free will without anyone's influence on it as in pressure which can come in , are we true to ourselves by selecting the right path by our free will of coming to a point without an second opinion is not at all fair from the third eye to see a pointless, effortless decision going into waste.

How can we stand alone against the world by fighting over our sole strength against the whole universe ?
I would rather say it will be very simple for an individual to decide what he/she has a needful amount of options in their hands, not by spilling it away in a useless manner , perhaps using it so it can give birth to many people's mindset of selecting their equal set of margin people.
It isn't fair for an individual to hold on to the rivalry for too long in his life , time is limited for everyone to spend on any living energy between differences of choices , irrespective of opinions , deflective voices.
If I start to lean on my shoulder to lean on for a while , relying on only my decision of what can be taken into implementation without any hesitation, our lives rather giving others to judge is a waste of energy and time.
Only we know of how far we have reached in this long journey, we would know our own potential of how to enact , react to uncontrollable turn around over a single day of living.
Instead i will say, ``Be good at assuming you are your own teacher, solution finder, decision maker, be kind to yourself when you have committed a mistake, let go of yourself and admit it just to you.
Choice is in your hands , decide by yourselves.

CHAPTER THIRTY-EIGHT

Fate/destiny

Whatever has to happen will happen. Even though we try our best to not put ourselves in that situation by keeping pushing ourselves over the line, it will happen without our knowledge , an identity crisis .

The energy, efforts we put in just to want the right set of person's in our lives, without any expectations while we set specific targets according to the milestones we would want to be travelled within a limited span of time in our lives as planned.

Both are unexpected in everyone's lives, it's not like we can decide which route we would want in that movement as in to let go of what we are doing and come over the situation we would be facing without any haste just as life throws in.

It's just easy for us as an individual to be ready in any given situation to face what may come in face by accepting , searching for an equivalent solution by trying to solve it with our bare mindfulness of ideas.

I/We should be ready at any given time for expecting anything best would happen according to the destination we would be going through a specific amount of a person life journey , it would end either in a successful journey without any hurdles including in it or it may have too many troubles such as complications, suffocations , emotions , sufferings, one sided feelings which will be turning into two - sided once in a while and go back into hiding such as tortoise.

Life isn't as expected for anyone especially who would want anything in their lives, one has to be very patient , focused on only one chart rather than drawing other charts , seeing their growth would be rather too much to look after. I would suggest one can focus on how much growth can be seen if you keep watering the only bar chart over a lot of sacrifices by giving up which you are not interested in or the bar charts which doesn't want to grow with you.

It is in our hands to write our own destiny, perhaps allowing fate to take our nonetheless actions which is being rested all along the way which can be very dangerous for a soft soldered human who is very attached to only a few things which can make him/her very much interested in the wholesome targets .

What can I do to be rightful to be established in others throughout careers , lives.

It isn't easy to let go of our dreams just in the world by throwing like garbage we do in the air, what sense can it make otherwise by fighting for what we love to do in our whole lot of aims which can take us to places either by the hard work , being consistent , loyal towards a single road of a single person soul to their heart.

It would be very easy for me , anyone just being there regularly , showing that you are not here to give up on your written destiny which you want to be in a specified life destination until their end of life together with the help of strength by showing how can you be so powerful just as a superhero , letting your guard down to achieving with very dream of sleeping it every day and night.

CHAPTER THIRTY-NINE

Inspiration

Everyone has someone in their lives by whom we get inspired by them and keep working towards our own life just to be successful , the person whom we follow is also well settled down with his own lifestyle so why wouldn't we also be at least at whatever level we can achieve in our efforts we can get enough of it.

There are few people who we get inspired , influenced by so that we would want to be that much accountable to get there one day with a whole lot of everyday putting all our soul into the work we are doing into it by not wanting any result perhaps just as a participant without any end result expectations.

It wouldn't be a shame for anyone to implement the similar lifestyle of living , it's not like we would follow it everyday without any originality but what can happen more than no accidents which we can control over it by being confident , controlling the incidents which wouldn't go over our boundaries.

By having someone whom we would love to watch and learn from the best to have similar kinds of stories which can kick start our journey with a bang can only influence us by doing the right amount of energy invested through a person.

It shall never conspire with us in whatever way we
would go to make us unworthy/useless in any way.
There are many more people who also inspire us , every
other person who travels through our life will tell us some
or the other way by their actions of acting towards their
self proclaimed way.
It will hit us with all the power with the realization
which can be more energized for us who would want to
put up our name in the uprising market which can be
transformed into a new world of only losers with winning
strategy by our own words of wisdom to struggle with lot
of enthusiasm, without giving up anything easily.
Majority of us wouldn't want to be unsuccessful , it isn't
an easy task for most of them to get through all their
demons inside having lots of battles killing each over for
the good over evil within.
Why it is so difficult for a living being to work on
specific ambitions which he would not be loving to do for
an environmental change within the soul , tells us that we
are not fit for this role without any self esteem .
As it's for our own good to not focus on the negative
energy rather transform all those fluctuations, sad feelings,
depressed thoughts , distressed emotions into a very well
versed positive energy which we can gather and put
around our mind and work towards the person whom we
want to be in our lives.

CHAPTER FORTY

Forgiveness

We all make mistakes , commit crimes for ourselves by not wanting to try , perhaps to run away from the problems which we would not want to face them it with our intentions being not in right place for an individual including me as not we are not any Supremes without any wholesome thoughts within ourselves just to kill the other person's mind with the regretless we would want to generate and ask for guilty to us.

By accepting for whatever it was intentionally , on purpose not wanting to achieve within the hierarchy of needs by a human just to satisfy their intentions , it would be more helpful for them to go on a run more than a walk with lots of doubts within their sufficient period of time.

We cannot get attached to only a similar lifestyle which shall bore us , interest on our own personal lives would be more get be less curious , be more furious without any consent of not letting go of our past mistakes which will be committed over the years with lot of regret , deepest condolences which shall turn us into mere a machine instead enjoying our daily establishments into living animals which we are , why cannot we deny by telling ourselves in a living consent.

It would rather take a great heart for one to let go of the opposite person's mistakes, wrong doings , by just accepting that we are not non thinking creatures just to get away with we didn't know of the mistakes which will be grieving in our souls without any other playing in our mind on repeat mode.

Why would be a better person of living in a fantasy world which shall change into a off world person without our concern into a different opinion , by letting our whole mindset into a single stored building , perhaps our mind should react, enact , respect with all we have got with full strength through the selected species which may overturn into a animal with no feelings, emotions , pain , no regret of accepting the rightful amount of sins which would cost us the loss in no effect.

It's not mandatory to be like one whom we intend to amplify all our intentions over the wrong side of selecting the things which would cost us all the winning streak against all the odds of losing the strong ends of our amends by degrading the best we have got.

In our strength , capacity of what we would have to endure the fullest of capacity to take over the grieving pain of thinking from their side of perception , why would they commit this type of sin which will create of ruckus in the end for us while we take a long leap into for a living without our constant effort to change into the other person , according to others expectations while we sit and relax back at our own dreams to archive it and come through it.

If it's not in our hands to change the shape of the result by taking the system, rightful energy into the soul of spirited one to change the living of their daily hell-bent activities by enabling our systems into leading some positive energy to them by brainstorming with heavy competition leading us through survival for fighting with our own family, any other livings .

Think it with lighter mind, your all network will be back at your hands just to enable our emotions which takes place at our own will back end with our permission rather by not allowing no one but ourselves with our whole soul into what we do the activities by not entering into the system of vervain filled nerves , can destroy the mortal bodies.

It's not easy for us to change or lifestyle of living by not allowing the people who committed all the hurtful mistakes just to make us to become weak while somewhere down the lane we are still struggling to find the peace which we are not finding it to maintain our answer to tell ourselves , of why was i targeted over millions.

Instead of consoling yourself everyday, give one more chance whom you have not yet forgiven.

They may still have their side of the answer to the situation causing the difficulties which you are still facing like a longtime warrant without any clarity of answer. Life is all about creating, finding the second chances , being rightful, grateful , watchful of mind full of conscious to be finding the balance between and not wanting to take over the vengeance to the person who had made you land in the first place but being thoughtful of not repeating the same mistake which the other person did in the back.

CHAPTER FORTY-ONE

Merciless

Human behaves , misbehaves more often than any other over even little things which may cause them heartfelt breakdown while in condition , in may not be that much concerned over the issue of acting without thinking of how the circumstances can change their intent by hurting deeply with lesser fact of instances without trusting a indefinite reason for putting ourselves in that situation.

We just go with the flow only by leading our selfish needs which are only required to lead the infrastructure and travel in our journey in the smoothest way without any hurdles , any distractions.

Why wouldn't others sacrifice their prejudice in our lives by enabling them to execute successfully in order for the projects which may take the lifetime dreams away from us in a single snap.

Without wasting any single second why wouldn't we want us to take all the freedom of sacrificing from what we are achieving in our personal lives by allowing us to be so annoying for people to discriminate against them , not to just make them so dead in every other way to just lowering their standards.

If we are allowing us to take all the limited establishments into consideration while we wouldn't lower all the standards which in ward go onto create a whole lot of problems which may not be cured through solutions which may or may not be found in the earliest of ages.

What would be a ruckus which is caused only by our actions towards a specified targeted person , later the same error will be repeating in every aspect of our lives just as often to hurt the other person feelings in just to amplify our perspective side of behavior, make fun of their perception without any knowledge of known well versed motions to enable our only words to be true.

While we believe that whatever we might try and intend for a rightful purpose might not end well if we are on the wrong side of the lane through worst of behavior including judging who would cause any change of plans in the decisions we intend to take.

From now on we shall stop making decisions which will hurt the other person ,as we would take a wrongful decision in haste .

With intention or without, being purposefully or non purposefully, it shouldn't make one person to get their standards low just because of our irrespective of thinking , words, actions into their lives will be disturbed and emotions will be broken down into small pieces of we existing them in the form of unworthy being , not trustworthy.

CHAPTER FORTY-TWO

Conscious mind and Subconscious mind:

What we think of the present , while we are awake in the reality of the universe .

Decisions which would be taken within our control by not allowing any others to get involved in any troubles or any misbelief which may land us into the most unspecified locations.

While we are out of the contrast of our mind control, the more deeply thing which we do without our control will be controlled by our subconscious mind , but rather it will make us do the right thing with the actions more than the words.

With whom we are more attached , enacting as if we wouldn't want to establish any relationship with them makes us go deeper into the dreams we wouldn't want in our reality but there will be more than enjoying their presence with the fullest of thoughts over taken by the happiness.

The more we try to make amends for all of the mistakes which would make us to regret by making our body weak, mind with lots of disturbance , makes us to think how we can be absurd by just a thought of not being in anyone's life as a special and share a unbreakable bond throughout in our lives.

It's not how you approach a person, but rather how you take along them through your journey and make them realize , be evergreen by giving our best to any kind of people we pass by.
While we would want all the people who are there in our subconscious mind to be present in our daily living to help us out by solving our problems , difficulties , enabling us to mingle with right amount of time to vibe with bunch of persons just for the safety of our mindset to achieve somewhat dreams which were left unturned in the first place while we had met before.
The more we don't the same people in our routine life which we wouldn't want to be in a repeated mode for whole year , as why wouldn't want to control all of them inside in our subconscious mind by not allowing them in our lives,
Why are we scared , what shall happen if they appear in your lifestyle
We are scared of losing people , the more we feel connected ; the more people who knows all our secrets would at last end up hurting the most in our lives , the more attached we get to them ; the more they would detached from us and later it would make us regretful for allowing them into the conscious mind and into the reality of our daily living.

CHAPTER FORTY-THREE

Curiosity

Why can't we be so eager to explore so many places in the globe to see what awaits us there ,what nature can give to us back while going to a specific destination.

How can't we control the excitement after meeting the most favorite person in our lives for the first time in the process of talking about whatever you had wished for long back when you were in your childhood.

What can be even told or not would be still left in the mystery to yourself of how to know their way of their world to understand them and get back to the reality and get adjusted to it.

It takes a lot of guts, glory will follow just as you start in your lifestyle to get along with whomever who you would want to spend time with , may take more than the time required to understand them , how would they react when they are in their ups and how badly will be there in downs.

It's all about trying your luck all the time , you wouldn't know at what time people shall start changing their way of taking decisions within their limit of life just to put to full stop of a new area while we would struggle to find a place to just survive.

We would be more keen on learning new aspects of adaptation , feelings, caring nature , how loyal they are to their friends, how they would apply themselves when in difficult situations by caring or reacting in a harsh way .

What kind of intention would be theirs to apply in everyone's lives just to switch from unknown strangers to the strongest of the relationships which will take them to the next place if we would want to exist in their heart and soul.

It will be more of a single sided boat which may drown into the ocean and people in it will die along with dreams of their would be permanently drowned along with the boat.

Just to apply ourselves far away from the enemies in us to fight them we would require a lot of less expectations rather just feeling of having a low key profile instead go into the society without any hesitation just for the self esteem for satisfying all our needs.

It would be better for us to stay grounded rather than being more extroverted in our lives, being more specific about our dreams, turning them into regretful .

Why wouldn't we wait for the right period of time to execute all the plans which we would want those things in our lives permanently? We can wait until there comes an emergency , by that time we would have got everything to explore with.

CHAPTER FORTY-FOUR

Responsibility

We always carry some amount of pressure which will be given by us for the living in this existence to prove ourselves on our shoulders , in order to satisfy and obey by the rules created by the society , by ourselves just to carry out specific roles which will be divided by our parents to represent a role which in later transformed into more serious one by our relatives just because we couldn't complete any milestone to the fullest by our ability.

It isn't so easy for a person to establish any kind of idea or physical tons of weightage pressure which will be expected by senior living family members in order to perform any kind of perfect planned achievement just to show it to our grandparents or to the neighbors, would be to relatives just to show off few dream over protected thoughts , desires.

To allow ourselves to go through many of our living goals , would take a lot of patience , due to the ongoing competition out in the world.

Once we are established , being famous, more of the expectations will be taken in to deliver more in the next upcoming sole projects which we would want to take up and perform again the next day, everyday there is a star that is born in the living.

People wouldn't remember who you are after you start giving your worst performances , perhaps they will only enjoy today's celebration even if it's a new concept to learn from it.

Life doesn't stand as we would want it to take a break from but would require new faces to replace the old ones by over taking the competition by its own pace with its own propaganda just to satisfy the new world as it is today by which we have equally wanted how it wants to be.

If you only want to take the burden to lead your family , it would take away all your freedom of network which you had in between your friends circle from the past, but what would you desire at the last matters the most until why would you settle for less , when you have diamonds in your hand , why chase for gold?

Don't go after chasing , even if it's your worth perhaps do your bit and leave how it is gradually it will only be realized by it's mistake and come back at you for not staying in your tendency of the circle which you had just built for them.

It is about how you generate strength from it rather than getting weak from it.

CHAPTER FORTY-FIVE

Naked/Mirror

We enter into this universe with a crying smile on our
face,
Our parents, relatives or any other people who see a
baby never complain about not wearing the dress,
The body of a baby which is always defined as a beauty
without clothes on!
Due to the pressure of society, we shall always be
judged on what attire we put on.
Perhaps society always complains!? Why!
This body of our soul is just a car to as a driver, Hence
it should be cleaned every time regularly and should be
kept regardless clean just as a car,
Human nature which evolves all around the world is in
the same cycle , as the tradition changes.
The aged people and the small babies are and always
will be put in a single category, because both of them
should be taken care of as "fragile".
They say love is blind, but they never say "Lust is
blind"? Right!
Love can only be felt mentally, not physically but it can
be sometimes not all the time©.
Comfortable we feel as we take a shower, with the
freedom of our full body to ourselves flying all over with a

background singer arising from our mouth.

The more naked we think through our thought process, the more effect shall happen over the end result.

The more complicated we start thinking, just as our dressing by we get influenced by them and start dressing by their interest. Our liberation of vision, hopes, dreams will be lost!

Let's start seeing through the blankness of life just as we see a naked body going down in a grave permanently, perhaps our life will get a fresh start just as the soul of an old body gets transmitted from one to another.

Happiness doesn't come just like that without any humiliation, Goals cannot be achieved without any sacrifices, Satisfaction comes only in the form of experiences of the past.

Rejection will always bring you next step closer to the "Acceptance", the more you think about what to think, when to think, and why to think, the more where you will think.

"Life is all about Representing, Organizing and Managing".

Think big, Live big, Dream big and Hope big with a small step everyday to a lifetime success!

What would make the mirror makes us to think every time we go in front of it , makes us to think the difference between us two of how the clean it is with its purity of the soul which makes us to tell the frankness of a person but makes us think why are humans act so fake from one person who is visible as pure from his clothes but from his actions why is he enacting a stage performance in reality of drama in everyday of his living.

It doesn't make sense to the mirror and asks the person , how good can you hide in front of other humans but in

front of me you are mere naked with all your intentions,
plans to play a drama in to people by making them as
emotional fools and making them rather as a doll with
your words of embarking untruthfulness , speech of only
unfair glory which will be only be true in it's own.
Why wouldn't we behave as a mirror to everyone while
we pass through some lifetime of journey by telling what
we feel, how we would want to express with our
straightness of thoughts just as plain.
What will it take for us to act , behave rightfully in our
lives from now on!
It would take a lot of guts, less of worry , leaving alone
of drama , untruthfulness by our selfish amends to enable
one of our dreams.

CHAPTER FORTY-SIX

Choice

Everyone has equal importance of pick through many options in whatever we can do in our daily essential lives just to pass through all the emotions which might hold back all the feelings, may break us and make us fall in the wrong direction in our lives just as to make the wrong amends , later on these will affect our actions every time when making a point to remember for others or ourselves.

It's about our equivalent set of right feelings come into one place , allowing us in taking the right option to pick up with the gut feeling adding some more fuel to our efficiency , by adding more confidence just to be sure of all the lifelong failures into one successful decisions which we are ready to take a whole lot of pressure to our mindset by selecting our instances right.

When in being irrespective of thoughts, fluctuating from one thought to another, be sure to take some inputs, opinions, reviews from your friends who are being accountable in your life just as a daily person to be sure of fullest.

Why wouldn't we be so uncertain about the choices we want to take in our lives just to be more than satisfied , more than happy than ever we wanted in our lives .

Distractions is taking away from us for the longing dream which we had made a roadmap of it's before even it had come in the existence in our lives but why aren't we making a delay for the action to take in just for the fear of losing the other person or the thing.

Fear of losing more than the love of gaining it's trust over us for the fullest with our utmost efforts including making the deal with the devil doesn't make much of difference just for the sake of short term bonding over understanding ourselves for the rest of our lives even without talking to each other.

It's not how many years we keep trying to achieve the specific target in our lives to accomplish , perhaps it's how long we have spent the time with it's internal behavior of our life between at the fullest of the emotions.

Why would it make a difference for a living species to prove ourselves just for the sake of doing it regularly with putting all our soul into it , sacrificing all our most important ingredient of love into for the gloaming purpose of it.

If not achieved with any less amount of energy within today's whole world population , competition and competitors are generating twice the smarter they are getting transformed .

The more quickly we take the actions to implement the plan which we had to execute, the further it must be put in place for now, for a better after and future.

The less friends you have in your circle , there would be less drama, more clarity, clear intentions with lots of helpful thoughts shared , planning the situation according to the life of how it progresses from time to time.

If we start believing in the process, progress will definitely follow, as we get along the trust we keep on the people should be kept loyal and later on should never be broken amongst anyone else.

Change is life , people keep changing their perspectives , feelings, emotions over the people whom they have lost in their life by regretting or not accepting and allowing them to settle down in the lifetime seat which is only for a special person.

We should start following a simple rule: any person can come into our lives and go whenever they want but remaining constant is yourself. We should be at least truthful , grateful , and meaningful just to show how much we love ourselves.

Promise

Suffer alone rather than sharing with less minded people sometimes,
Share your experience not plans and dreams with anyone as neither one time or many times,
Taste the success like a emperor and celebrate it like a victory of festival! "Every time"
Many times people come through your mind and influence you as well as inspire you. Perhaps you start to behave and enact like them, 'sometimes'.
We always think from our empathy that their lives are better than us, but many times we forget even if they are mortal just like us and they shall also fall and fail in life and get hurt.
The more we start comparing ourselves to others, the more times we start degrading ourselves nonetheless!
Sometimes it's better to be selfish and enjoy few things in few days on our own,
Many times the mistakes we make the more experienced and more we regret and learn that it should not be repeated next time.
Sometimes we feel being alone is better as an "Introvert" but many times situations don't allow us and turns us automatically into "Extrovert".

Many times people who come into our life always teach us at least a single lesson each, let's not forget that as in many of us forget it.
A lot of temporary people would teach us "many times" not to get attached with every person you cross paths with!
"Sometimes" people whom we don't expect that we would share a good bond with become one of our closest in our lives!
It's not easy for a person just to promise to themselves , go according to the plan that they wished to travel in the diversity of many ambitions , primary contacts which they would get more attention through lots of pain , disrespect , with a lot of gut feeling.
It's like being in your zone by giving up all artificially you liked better than walking towards you love the most in your life by not attending any specific attendance with less of your soul interested to do that work , but your soul would be more itching to do some other work which you would not worried to work your intentions at the rightful place with lots of positive vibes would come in.
How can you be so liberal by accounting to the same mistake by grieving to accept our only regret by imagining the whole intention of not allowing anyone near us through the same meaningful pain, agony , disrespectful , meaningless connections, relationships which we are in with toxic , useless unwanted conversations throughout.
We would like to be a part of someone's life, but?
The door to their soul is closed, as even though we keep trying to open it up with duplicate keys,
With the help of key maker just as we approach a third person to fix our issues rather than open it with the spare

key with what we have,
Some people simply sit whole throughout the day, sleep
tight with alcohol in their body as they just spectate for
today's, tomorrow's and regret the "yesterday" they lost.
Many just through the life as in a circle just to keep
getting onto the next things in their life, will be rotating in
same format just as earth is rotating every day,
Very few are adapting on, learning new skills, and
attitude towards life as of now.
"We are after all just humans"!
Dramebaaz we are in every topic, as we change the
situation, topic, answer according to our requirements and
perspectives so we can be safer.
We bleed, we die, we are born again, but the joy in our
life span is not enjoyed by everyone, as we shouldn't lose
any small happy moment.
There is no second chance for us to prove as in to
anyone, so let's be clear of our actions, words, behavior of
what we want to do in our individual lives.
Life's too short to think about what we are going to be,
why we are doing it, which one with which I'm living my
life, where I want to be in my future.
Spend less, invest more, Make few true friends rather
than 1000 followers on social platforms.
Nothing matters lasts forever as an ocean, even if it
requires rain from the clouds such as us to live. We also
require love in another perception.
We should evaporate just like the ocean to clouds and
help the people who are in difficult situations.
Move on, never stay in one place because each place
has that very own vibe.
Learn from your mistakes, until you learn the mistakes
keep repeating.

Listening to a lot of people, what they have to say and their perspectives, thoughts, reasons, experiences may tell you something.

Love all, hate none!?

Execution is the main part in our lives, many fail here because of fear of failure, loss of their identity, the more you fear, the more you fail.

The more you imply all of this in a right person, thing. The end result will definitely take place in its own way.

Our life is just as the food we order to the waiter after seeing the options which we may get in our lives,

We only get what we order,

Rest all mustn't be preferred ,

The first time when we get an opportunity in life must be seized , same as when the waiter delivers the starter to us.

While riding, never complain by honking , rather accept that the vehicle wouldn't want to leave you in that specified pathway , searching for a different way to go.

In life it's not fair to blame everything on others , put all your problems on your shoulders and carry on saying I solved my own problem.

We never tell the whole truth to anyone , even to the closed ones in our life , perhaps change the whole story and tell it according to our perspective just to save ourselves from the reactions society might show to us.

CHAPTER FORTY-EIGHT

Warranty/Guarantee

What would an individual give their lifelong trust by enabling full interest of life to any person in the life span of living to the earnest, a product which can be labelled with minimum years of span within to hold on to all the problematic situations in which it can undergo very less certain damage in its range and limit.

Enabling anyone to live through most of us giving at whatever we are best should be willing to enlighten the youth to follow the right path of up gaining freedom of selection and their own individuality for their right of living.

If we are able to live by ourselves without changing our lifestyle , attitude towards how we behave in different and difficult situations also helps us to come through by people where they would be trusting us more than themselves.

There comes a time choosing the right option between the two difficult meaningful , worthless positions of the rightful amount of time , money which is invested through many appearances but the same amount of problems would arise in our lives accordingly.

Why aren't we believing anything which is already in the early phase of our lives , is enchanting behind our ears with a loud voice as we are moving forward with the wrong accusations in our names even though the villain remains unnamed and unmasked.

The enjoyment of their success is being celebrated , well versed, arranged into anything which can be very disguised into which previous was a meaningful one in both the lives respectfully.

How good the bond may be , the strongest will be broken soon into pieces due to the eyes of many will be on them.

What should be done to safeguard all the meaningful lessons, memories , beautiful moments that went in vain ?

One should be on the losing side to keep losing to the other person , to gain their lifetime warranty upon us to trust us blindly until then keep pushing , trying to up your game higher. That's it, keep repeating it. Shhhhhhhhhhhhhhhhhh, it's a secret to keep it to yourself.

In our daily life we pass through few people whom we had met them in our early life,

Life's a journey where we keep travelling towards a specific goal but as we go ahead , a bunch of similar travelers meet across our journey and move out.

They share their life experience, expectations, achievements, goals, dreams , ambition towards life which makes us more curious to know about it rather than looking after ourselves,

We always want an escape pass from our friends, relatives, new people whom we meet and run away from our daily struggles and hustle so we can stay calm and enjoy today, perhaps regretting about wasting now,
Our life's journey can't or will not be explained to everyone every time, coz life's not to share. It is about how you live, not lie.
But as we humans always want more from everyone whom we have in our life, perhaps that's why we all are selfish in one way or another, if we are not selfish, life will make us be .
It's survival of the fittest not about encouraging who won , yes we do that most of the time rather focusing on what went wrong with our own performance, perspective and personally work towards it.
Acknowledging it , I can say we are not selfless why? Sometimes we do react as animals, let's not forget that we belong to animal species,
We stop caring for the people whom we love the most, we hate the people who love us the most, it's all about picking the correct option in our lives but why do we fail every time when we pick something up.
Life's very short to hold grudges, make friends, believe in miracles it will take time, good connections, respect and value family, don't lose your hope , fight for what you love and remember just never give up on all these things to live a beautiful living life, trust me you will not regret it.
The one who sacrifices everything for his goal towards his/her success overcomes lot of hurdles in his individual life independently more often by his own identity,
The one who loses also does the same, but it's life right, everyone can't be on the winning side.

Some has to lose even though they are deserving but few turn out to be a winner towards their specific goal, It's totally all right to keep losing in life because the more you fail and fall , the more you gain experience from losing and will never come in the same path as you attempted last time , will tell others also of how to approach.

The more often you lose you look back to the basics of what's wrong, work more, stop worrying about others because you will be more reliable and concentrate more on your efforts, causes and the effects.

I am not being an empathetic person or a writer telling you to lose or to be negative, it's just that we all want to win in our lives, be successful, be as rich as possible, but life doesn't go according to our plans right?

Life is not about worrying about the future or regretting what you did in your past , perhaps the future is today.

What you do for today and now will reflect your life , develop in your life in upcoming.

No one will come and pick you up if you have fallen down, sympathy will be shown from them but no help will be done .

Get up on your own legs, walk , run, sprint at your own pace, don't worry about competition and remember never get influenced by anyone and increase your pace .

Be in your own zone and approach your main goal.

Winners never think of anything, their perspective will be from one side thinking but the society, family loves to hear or watch the success stories of them , not that they were successful . It's just that they were famous so they can tell their friends, family that they heard or watched them or their story.

Remember no one likes or hears the story of runner up or losing guy/girl , society only accepts who are famous as winners.

Keep working towards it , you may not know at what time your opportunity comes knocking on your door, consistency is mandatory and being loyal towards it is compulsory.

Response, Reply ,Request, Responsibility. Remember those four "R" will only be given to you when you are rightfully angry with revengeful success in your life.

You decide who you want to become? Keep winning? Trying , failing and to be successful!??

CHAPTER FORTY-NINE

Forever

"Forever is a beautiful lie which will destroy us in the end". Which bond in nowadays will exist nonetheless which has no strings in their shall last long which has no meaningful name to that relationship without any intention to be one great understanding forever and ever.

If you have the person in your hands to take care of , still misunderstanding will take place over the influential people who would want to overcome the cheap politics over their selfish needs or fear of losing their trusted aid group or gang.

They cannot withstand anything which can come in their way as an obstacle in order to avoid their bonding over the new set of people.

The memory will not fade away in anyone's brain , it might be deleted in their phone memory but in the wholesome of the mind it's very rare to get deleted.

It doesn't fade away as easily as we would be thinking , what another way we can think to get back to making them realize whatever thinking they had over the meaning of the forever must be proven wrong.

You have to conquer the world to show the universe
your potential of how much you can take up your people
into your lives personally , especially after facing a lot of
criticism under the name of love, marching towards the
lone victory of freedom by thoughts just to make all her
dreams into reality.
Accepting and moving on in the way they have shown
you in life that you are still going ahead without any
targeted device to be found in the rightful path to the soul
which you have been trying to get in touch with your
dream.

"No one will help no one"
Everyone are scared because of that someone will take
their place of life which they are living under,
We have to come up in our lives "individually", some
may inspire you, few may influence you, many will
discourage you.
Everyday, everybody, everyone will start becoming
selfish, perhaps bringing scare to the people by telling the
hustle and struggle.
'The competition for them would become very thin, the
race would be also of less individuals'.
Never, ever forget that for what you have come here till
now, for whom you travelled so far the journey, for why
you have sacrificed so much to achieve your specific goal.
Everybody hates everybody, we are all just mortal fools
who just dress up nicely, act fiercely without mercilessly
and enact it again by defining it sarcastically! Is it?
An ant I saw on the land where it was fighting for
survival between the humans walking over it,

The outcasts are also merely surviving under the domination over the higher level of people who are controlling their every step with the power of money and influence.

As a cow, we humans wander just like them without any specific goal in our mind, the intention of moving towards an ideal pathway working to a cause so the end result shall also be taken, but many of them have no idea.

How to draw your own dreams, even did but which one to follow.

'Confused of choosing this one or that one, no let me do both. Shall I do the new dream which I got now, wait let me think!'

Should I start now, today or tomorrow?

What if I fail and surrender to the life where I should get adjusted to?

Better begin it now or never!

Failed. No problem, try it again from your experience last time.

"Do it again but do it way better, the more you keep on trying, the less the competition and competitors! ".

The long run winners never worry about the rejection they receive or get, the only thing that matters for them is the win which awaits and brings the joy of entering the heaven gate.

"Everyone is busy with their own problems and people struggle with their own life".

Life's not permanent just as the people who travel across your journey, they are just a spectator. Merely knows the pathway of how you walked till now or who you are going through this process.

Take along the opportunity to carry people's opinions, perspectives and suggestions, but at last your decision must be independently decided.

Many may come, most of them may go, but few will always stay in your life. Appreciate that they are willing to stay by your side rather than pushing away from yourselves.

Journey is endless, Experience is limitless, Mistakes are countless, Time is priceless, Results are worthless because life is mortal less.!

CHAPTER FIFTY

Motivation

In one's life without any motivation we wouldn't be even keep moving forward in our lives , it's the daily process we do by getting motivated who inspires us everyday just by their actions, disciplines which they follow every day , rules , boundaries which they have implemented to not go out of their role by not putting any of their business.

That's what makes them stand out , be famous in their personally selected field of interest by not allowing more people into their mind nor taking too much pressure from the outside world.

They maintain a well balanced lifestyle in between their personal and professional careers of which they keep certain barriers in between so it wouldn't collide and create any problem over the two set of lives.

There are many individuals who follow the same path but in between get distracted over lack of consistency , intensity of problems which arise over the levels of oceans through our lives.

It may take a little while for us all to realize , real intention of how we can be daily motivated . Just look out near you there is so much in nature and people to get motivated , hear your instinctive voice telling you something after you have missed something spectacular to aim at.

If you are not motivating yourself , no one else will
perhaps all are busy in their lives.
Being human is all about representing, organizing,
managing , engaging.
You always have a choice , the selection is in your
hands to select the right path to lead on and inspire
someone who can go ahead and achieve what they gladly
want to become.
Life is all about finding the right balance, solutions by
taking meaningful decisions.
Your problem is your problem, no one else's.
The biggest of the battles takes place in yourself/inside
your heart and your mind.
The more you start caring about what others think, the
more you start getting weaker from inside .
The closer you stay, the more painful it gets.
More far you prefer to stay, the closer you become,
If you are not doing it now, you are never doing it later.
Life is a journey, not a destination!
It only matters how you travel , not where to.
We may be the masters of our thoughts, but we are not
slaves to our emotions and feelings.
Sometimes when we find love, we push it away without
knowing the value of it by ignoring it.
No matter who you are , no matter what you have done,
no matter where you come from, you can always change.
A lot of drama could be avoided if more people just
learned how to not react to the acquisitions which they are
not their own.
Differences is all that matters, people who search for
life end up with nothing or something.

Everyone will have the same life but the difference will be who stands out with yourself with accepting of difference.
The tomorrow is coming here anytime soon. Be ready and prepared for it now.
Love is not the colliding of two bodies, it is of colliding 2 souls into one.
Stop asking, start getting , spread giving.

About The Author

My previous books : Mind in several humans,
Love is all I need ,
And I returned from my death only for you
My blog page: https://wordpress.com/view/
akkiwritesblog.wordpress.com
My Twitter account: Amarnath Akki-45
My email id: amarca683@gmail.com

9 798888 569124 6